KHANIQAHI-NIMATULLAHI (NIMATULLAHI SUFI ORDER)

306 West 11th Street
New York, New York 10014
Tele: 212-924-7739

4021 19th Avenue
San Francisco, California 94132
Tele: 415-586-1313

4931 MacArthur Blvd. NW
Washington, D.C. 20007
Tele: 202-338-4757

84 Pembroke Street
Boston, Massachusetts 02118
Tele: 617-536-0076

310 NE 57th Street
Seattle, Washington 98105
Tele: 206-527-5018

11019 Arleta Avenue
Mission Hills, Los Angeles, California 91345
Tele: 213-365-2226

4642 North Hermitage
Chicago, Illinois 60640
Tele: 312-561-1616

405 Greg Avenue
Santa Fe, New Mexico 87501
Tele: 505-983-8500

219 Chace Street
Santa Cruz, California 95060
Tele: 408-425-8454

41 Chepstow Place
London W.2. England
Tele: 01-229-0769

Spiritual Poverty in Sufism

Also available by Dr. Javad Nurbakhsh:

1. In the Tavern of Ruin: Seven Essays on Sufism
2. In the Paradise of the Sufis
3. What the Sufis Say
4. Masters of the Path
5. Divani Nurbakhsh: Sufi Poetry
6. Sufism: Meaning, Knowledge and Unity
7. Traditions of the Prophet, Vol. I
8. Sufism: Fear and Hope, Contraction and Expansion, Gathering and Dispersion, Intoxication and Sobriety, Annihilation and Subsistence
9. The Truths of Love: Sufi Poetry
10. Sufi Women
11. Traditions of the Prophet, Vol.II
12. Jesus in the Eyes of the Sufis

Spiritual Poverty in Sufism

(Faqr & Faqir)

Including some definitions of
Spiritual Stations,
Mystical States,
Time,
and Breath.

by

Dr. Javad Nurbakhsh

KHANIQAHI-NIMATULLAHI PUBLICATIONS
LONDON

SPIRITUAL POVERTY IN SUFISM

by Dr Javad Nurbakhsh

Translated by Leonard Lewisohn
Design by Jane Lewisohn
ISBN 0-933546-11-4

Published by Khaniqahi-Nimatullahi Publications
London

Address: 41 Chepstow Place
London W.2
Telephone: 01-229-0769

Printed by Morning Litho Printers in Great Britain (T.U.)

CONTENTS

ABBREVIATIONS

Below is the list of works often cited in the text. Bibliographical and publishing data on the various works can be found in the bibliography at the back of the book.

AT	*Asrâr at-tauḥid*
AN	*Asrâr-nâma*
AA	*Aurâd al-aḥbâb wa foṣuṣ al-âdâb*
AM	*'Awâref al-ma'âref*
B	*Bustân-e Sa'di*
EO	*Eḥyâ-ye 'olum-e din*
ES	*Eṣṭelâhât as-ṣufiyah* ('Abdo'r-Razzâq Kâshâni)
FJ	*Fawayeḥ al-jamâl' was fawateḥ al-jalâl*
G	*Golestân-e Sa'di*
HA	*Haft Aurang*
HH	*Ḥadiqat al-ḥaqiqat*
HS	*Ḥâlât wa sokhanân Abu Sa'id Abe'l-Khair*
JS	*Jâme' ṣaghir*
KF	*Kashshâf eṣṭelâḥat al-fonun*
KM	*Kashf al-maḥjub*
KST	*Kholâsa-ye sharḥ-e ta'arrof*
KS	*Kimiyâ-ye sa'âdat*
LT	*Loma' fe't-taṣawwof* (Ketâb al-)
M	*Mojli*
MAS	*Majmu'a-ye âthâre-e fârsi-ye Shaikh al-Eshrâq*
MAr	*Manâqeb al-'ârefin*
MA	*Mashrab al-arwâḥ*
ME	*Merṣâd al-'ebâd*
MH	*Meṣbâḥ al-hedâyah*
MM	*Mathnawi-ye ma'nawi*
MR	*Majmu'a-ye Resa'il Khwâja 'Abdo'llâh Anṣâri*
MS	*Manâzel as-sâ'erin*
NO	*Nafahât al-ons*
NrO	*Nur al-'olum*

RA	*Resa'il Khwâja 'Abdo'llah Anṣâri*
RQ	*Resâla-ye Qoshairiya*
RSh	*Resâlahâ-ye Shâh Ne'mato'llâh Wali*
SB	*Safinat al-baḥâr*
SM	*Ṣad Maidân*
SS	*Sharḥ-e shaṭḥiyât-e* (Ruzbehân)
TA	*Tadhkerat al-auliyâ'*
TfA	*Tafsir-e 'erfâni wa adabi-ye Qor'ân-e majid*
TKQ	*Tarjoma-ye kalâmât-e qeṣâr-e Bâbâ Ṭâher*
TJ	*Ta'rifât-e Jorjâni*
TS(A)	*Ṭabaqât aṣ-ṣufiyyah* (Anṣâri)
TS(S)	*Ṭabaqât aṣ-ṣufiyyah* (Solami)
TT	*Taṣawwof wa adabiyât-e taṣawwof* (includes: *Mer'ât-e 'oshâq)*

PREFACE

In the Name of the Exalted and the Sacred

Time and time again, it has been brought to my attention that many sufis are unversed in their own terminology, unacquainted with the definitions of such elementary terms as *faqir, darvish,* and *ṣufi.* We have endeavoured to shed light on these concepts in the first three essays of this volume.

In a previous book[1], various definitions of 'Sufi' and Sufism *(taṣawwof)* as provided by the classical Sufi teachers, were presented. Further definitions recently discovered are given here, as well.

In conclusion, a few additional terms which sufis who are on the Path should be aware of, are analysed. These include an enquiry into the meanings of *ḥâl* (mystical state), *maqâm* (spiritual station), *waqt* (time), and *nafas* (breath).

It is hoped that this collection will serve to deepen their comprehension of these matters, and inspire them on the Way.

Dr. Javad Nurbakhsh

1. *Sufism: Meaning Knowledge, and Unity* (N.Y. 1981) pp.11-44

TRANSLITERATION EQUIVALENTS

Arabic Alphabet	Latin Alphabetic Equivalents	Pronounciation of Unfamiliar Sounds
Consonants		
ء أ	'	Glottal stop, as at the beginning of any English word which starts with a vowel
ب	b	
ت	t	
ث	th	th — As in '**th**ink' — unvoiced (Arabic); simply s in Persian
ج	j	
ح	ḥ	
خ	kh	kh — Guttural as German or Scottish **ch**
د	d	
ذ	dh	dh — As in '**th**e' — voiced (Arabic); simply **z** in Persian
ر	r	r — Trilled as Italian initial **r**
ز	z	
س	s	
ش	sh	
ص	ṣ	ṣ — In Arabic: a slurred **ṣ** with sides of tongue curved up against palate; in Persian: normal **s**
ض	ḍh	ḍh — In Arabic: sides of tongue curved up as with preceding letter but with tip touching back of front teeth;
ط	ṭ	
ظ	ẓ	
ع	'	

Arabic Alphabet	Latin Alphabetic Equivalents
غ	gh
ف	f
ق	q
ک	k
ل	l
م	m
ن	n
و	w
ه	h
ی	y
ة	h,t,a*

Added Persian Consonants

پ	p
چ	ch
ژ	zh
(as **z** in 'siezure')	
گ	g
(hard as in 'got')	

Vowels

Long

آ	â
اُو	u
اِی	i

Short

اَ	a
اُ	o
اِ	e

Diphthongs

اَو	au
اَی	ai

	in Persian:	normal **z**
ṭ	In Arabic:	middle of tongue touching tip of front teeth;
	in Persian:	normal **t**
ẓ	In Arabic:	sides of tongue curved up and touching teeth on either side of front teeth;
	in Persian:	normal **z**
ʻ	In Arabic:	sound made by tightening of throat;
	in Persian:	glottal stop, like first letter of alphabet above
gh	In Arabic:	rolled guttural, as French **r;**
	in Persian	a guttural stop, similar to Arabic but not rolled
q	In Arabic:	like a swallowed **k** — unvoiced;
	in Persian:	same as Persian **gh** — voiced

* (last letter of Arabic feminine singular nouns:
if h, noun in a final position;
if t, noun in liaison with following word;
if a, noun represented in a Persian title or text
[like Latin, Spanish or Italian feminines ending in -a used in English, which, like Persian, does not feature grammatical gender])

Note: 1) Arabic first names of Moslems (of Persian or whatever origin) are represented in fully elided forms to facilitate pronunciation for the English-speaking reader (examples:

عبد الرحيم Abdo'r-Raḥim,
فريد الدين Farido'd-Din).

(This is the only instance where Arabic nominal inflections are represented.) 2) The l of the Arabic article ال (al-) is shown in its conjunct form with the 'solar' letters succeeding it (example:

التوحيد at-tauḥid);

otherwise, the transliteration represents the written form common to both Arabic and Persian rather than the variant Persian pronunciation forms (which are indicated in the pronunciation note with each letter having a variant sound).

TRANSLATOR'S NOTE

The Persian original of this book was issued under the title of *Faqr Va Faqir* by Khaniqahi Nimatullahi Publications in London, 1982. References to the classical doctrinal works on Sufism are all paginated whenever possible, with the exception of *Divans,* which the scholarly reader may easily trace by referring to the rhyme-word of the original Persian distich in any of the printed editions.

فقر و فقیر

1

Spiritual Poverty

Spiritual Poverty

Since
The mansion of monotheism,
Divine Unity's[1] house, was built
firmset on the foundation of spiritual poverty,
of ego-annihilation[2],
Only on such foundation
Should this structure be up-raised.

Maghrebi, *Diwân*

'Poverty' *(faqr)* signifies destitution, impoverishment, and neediness, as contrasted to 'wealth' *(ghanâ),* which connotes 'independance' and 'self-sufficiency'. Poverty is in reality a devotee's attribute, whereas wealth is an attribute of the Lord. In this sense, the Qoran declares: "O Mankind! You are poor in relation to God, and God is the Rich, the Glorious". (XXXV: 15)

The term 'poverty' has various meanings:

1. Sometimes poverty implies straightened circumstances and material need. In this case, the word *faqir* ('poor one', 'pauper') means only a beggar, in contradistinction to *meskin* ('one who is lowly and destitute'). A distinction is often made

1. *Tauḥid*
2. *Fanâ*

between the two, insofar as a *faqir* is considered to be a *darvish* who has the ability to support himself and spouse for a few days, whereas the *meskin* is someone afflicted by extreme need and impoverishment.

2. Sometimes poverty implies an individual's spiritual impoverishment and need for God. In this case, the term *faqir* has different shades of meaning, as follows:

a. synonymous with the ascetic *(zâhed),* who renounces the world to attain a reward in the hereafter.

synonymous with the *ṣufi,* who renounces both this world and the next to attain the Truth. Here, the term *faqir* is identical in meaning to the Perfect Man *(ensân-e kâmel)* and the sufi who has attained total mystical reabsorbment *(fanâ)* in the Truth. All references to poverty and *faqir* in this book are with this connotation. As Ḥâfeẓ in verse has sung:

O God, grant me
the riches of poverty
for in such largesse lies
my power and glory.

The *Faqir* and Poverty in the *Qoran*

The main verses mentioning poverty in the *Qoran* are as follows:

1. "Satan promises you poverty *(faqr).*" (II: 268)
2. "Alms are for the poor *(foqarâ)*[1] and the

1. Arabic plural of *faqir*

needy *(masâkin).*"[1] (IX: 60)

3. "If you manifest your almsgiving, it is well, but if you hide it and give it to the poor *(foqarâ),* it is better for you." (II: 271)
4. "Alms are for the poor *(foqarâ)* who are constrained in the way of God, and are unable to travel in the land." (II: 273)

All the above verses refer to poverty and *faqirs* only in the context of material neediness.

5. "O mankind! You are the poor *(foqarâ)* in your relation to God, and God is the Rich, the Praiseworthy." (XXXV:15)
6. "And God is Rich, and you are poor." (XLVII:38)
7. "So Moses wattered their flocks for them.[2] Then he turned aside into the shade, and said; "My Lord I am needy *(faqir)* of whatever good thou sendest down for me." (XXVIII: 24)

These last three references to the term *faqir* are synonymous with the term *ṣufi,* who is an adherent of the way of Spiritual Poverty.

Traditions of the Prophet[3]
Concerning Spiritual Poverty

Poverty is a central theme in these sayings ascribed to Moḥammad:

1. Arabic plural of *meskin*
2. The two daughters of Sho'aib (or Jethro in the Old Testement) one of whom Moses later married.
3. *Ḥadith.* See also the second volume of the author's *Traditions of the Prophet.* (New York: 1984)

1. "Poverty is my pride and I glory in it".

SB, II, p. 378

Hâj Mollâ Hâdi Sabzewâri the 19th century Iranian philosopher, annotated this saying with this verse:

This is clear proof enough for me
of poverty's real wealth:
that it was the pride of the Prophet,
master of the pilgrims of poverty.

2. "Poverty is shame-facedness[1] in this world and the next".

SB,II, p. 378

The esoteric interpretation of this tradition is that the human being is 'possible being'.[2] Without the 'Necessary Being', (i.e. God) the human being has no existence; that is to say, his existence in its contingency is in need of the 'Necessary Being'. Thus the existential poverty of his 'possible being' culminates in 'shamefacedness' and disgrace in this world and the next.

Maghrebi, in the following verses, interprets this tradition:

If you don't know anything about that 'black face',
here and hereafter...
Open your eyes, look at the blackness of

1. Literally: black-facedness; a favourite simile of the sufi poets.
2. This statement is based on the propositions and terminology of Avicennan philosophy in which 'possible being' denotes creation in the sense that it is contingent on God's will and hence, may or may not be. The 'Necessary Being' however, denotes that Being which is self-caused and must be (i.e. God).

our poverty, our infamy.
The infamy of vanity is shrouding
the Absolute Reality with your ego.
But Truth's pure infamy, O genius, is
concealment of selfhood in Truth.
As long as you're self-fixated and bound
by your ego, you veil Reality.
What of our infamy can you fathom
fettered by such infamy?

3. "Poverty approaches the point of infamy."

JS, Vol. 2, p. 88

The esoteric interpretation of this tradition is that when the *faqir* attains a state of complete self-negation, absolutely no need is sensed for anything at all. Here one, in the words of a Sufi shaikh, may even exclaim, "The true *faqir* has no need of God". Such expressions are, of course, considered blasphemous by ordinary people. However, in the view of the gnostics and saints, the *faqir* who becomes annihilated in the essence and attributes of the Divine, actually does not exist, much less have need for anything. In the words of 'Aṭṭâr:

In the land of infamy
The mystic pitches his tent,
dressed in the vestment of "poverty
approaches a point..." and secluded from the rabble
by a "blackened visage here and hereafter".

4. "Poverty is glory to its possessor."

KM (orig.) p. 23

"The Doctors of the Mystic Path are not agreed as to the respective merits of Poverty *(faqr)* and Purity *(ṣafwât)*. Some hold that Poverty is more perfect than Purity. Poverty, they say is complete annihilation in which every thought ceases to exist, and Purity is one of the 'stations' *(maqamât)* of Poverty: when annihilation is gained all 'stations' vanish into nothing... Those who set Purity above Poverty say that Poverty is an existent thing and is capable of being named, whereas Purity is the being pure *(ṣafâ)* from all existing things; *ṣafâ* is the essence of annihilation *(fanâ)*, and Poverty is the essence of subsistence *(baqâ)*: therefore Poverty is one of the names of the 'waystations', but Purity is one of the names of Perfection."

KM, (trans) p. 58

The *Faqir* and Spiritual Poverty According to the Masters

In no book, no record, can
the lore of poverty be stored,
nor reckoning of love
be rendered on doomsday.

'Aṭṭâr

1. Khwâja 'Abdo'llâh Anṣâri: "Poverty is a *simorgh*[1] of which the name alone remains. It is subject to no one's control. The *faqir* is a madman,

1. A fabulous bird in Persian mythology, considered to be the Lord of all other fowls.

poverty is sanity. Poverty is a door and the *faqir* a house. Poverty is a waystation and a Divine mystery, into it no path leads, of its reality no one is aware."

RA, p. 136

2. Anṣâri: "Poverty is the red sulphur, the green elixir[1] which through striving cannot be acquired."

RA, p. 137

3. Anṣâri: "Know that there are two varieties of poverty. One, against which the Prophet of God cautioned, when he said, "In You I seek asylum from poverty". Concerning the other he commented, "Poverty is my pride". The former approaches impiety, the latter, Reality. The poverty resembling impiety pertains to the heart; it deprives the heart of all knowledge *('elm)*, wisdom *(ḥekmat)*, virtue *(akhlâq)*, patience *(ṣabr)*, contentment *(redhâ)*, humble submission *(taslim)*, and trust *(tawwakol)* in God, until from all these higher states it is impoverished... But that poverty of the Spirit which the Prophet deemed an honour, is that which divests a man of worldliness and approximates him to true piety or real faith".

TfA, II, p. 516

4. Shah Ne'mato'llâh: "Initially poverty is renunciation of the world and all in it; ultimately it is annihilation *(fanâ)* in the Essence of the Integration of the Oneness".

RSh, IV, p. 177

1. Alchemical symbols metaphorical of spiritual transmutations.

5. Abu 'Ali Daqqâq: "The greatest of all things is to abide in the expanse of poverty, and to competely abandon travelling the horizons, till in this way one possesses neither home nor whereabouts, neither money nor property."

He was questioned, "Is there no remuneration for someone who acquires these qualities?".

"What people wear, he also wears," he replied, "what they eat he eats, yet in his innermost consciousness *(serr)* he is disassociated from them."

TA, p. 656

6. "In the year 1003 or 1004 a darvish came to meet Master Abu 'Ali from Zuzan. He wore a sackcloth coat and a woolen cap. One of our brothers tried to humour him, and asked, "How much did you buy that sackcloth for?" He rejoined, "I purchased it for the sum of the world. I was offered the hereafter in exchange, but refused to trade."

RQ, p. 454

7. Shaikh Abu 'Ali recounted, "A would-be *faqir* stood up in a Sufi assembly and petitioning those present, said: 'I haven't eaten a morsel for three days" '.

"You are a liar," retorted a Sufi master who was present; "poverty is a Divine mystery, and God does not let his mysteries lie about for people to reveal."

RQ, p. 454

8. Abu Moḥammad Rowaim, upon being asked about poverty, replied, "It is yielding up the body to

God's bidding".

RQ, p. 454

9. Explaining the qualities of the *faqir,* Rowaim said: "The *faqir* is one who keeps his secret, is vigilant over himself, and performs God's commands".

TA, p. 484

10. Rowaim: "There is majesty in poverty which requires that it remain hidden, inviolate and jealously protected. Whoever divulges it, and flaunts it before people ceases to belong to this company, and has no eminence in poverty."

NO, p. 97

11. Rowaim, when asked of the reality of poverty, replied: "To select things justly, and when needy, to choose the lesser over the more."

TS(S), p. 182

12. Ebrâhim Qaṣṣâr: *"Foqarâ* have a certain raiment, which when consummately worn, bears the fruit of contentment."

RQ, p. 454

13. Ḥamdun Qaṣṣâr: "The natural state of the *faqir* is humility. If he becomes proud of his poverty, he surpasses all the wealthy in pride."

TA, p. 403

14. Ḥamdun Qaṣṣâr: "The eminence of the *faqirs'* rank is in humility. If he forsakes humility, he abandons all other virtues as well."

TA, p. 403

15. Jonaid: "Poverty is emptying the heart of forms."

TA, p. 445

16. Jonaid: "Poverty is a sea of affliction."

TA, p. 445

17. Jonaid: "Whenever you meet a *faqir,* deal indulgently with him. Don't start a conversation with him about knowledge *('elm)* for it will only intimidate him. Showing him consideration and indulgence, however, will persuade him to be sympathetic towards you."

TS, p. 160

18. Morta'esh recounted; "I asked Jonaid, 'Can a *faqir* really be disconcerted by knowledge?' He replied, 'Yes indeed. The *faqir,* sincere in poverty, melts away like lead in fire, if knowledge is mentioned to him.' "

RQ, p. 460-461

19. Jonaid: "The sign of sincere *faqirs* is that they do not ask questions, and do not dispute. If someone else argues with them, they remain silent."

TA, p. 444

20. Abu 'Abdo'llâh Moḥammad ebn Khafif: "Poverty is privation of possessions, and passing away from the self's qualities."

RQ, p. 461

21. Abu 'Abdo'llâh Khafif: "The Sufi is one whom God chooses for Himself out of His love, and the *faqir* is one who chooses poverty for himself in order to come close to Truth."

MH, p. 118

22. Asked for the 'sign of poverty' Kharaqani replied, "That the heart be black." 'Meaning what?' he was questioned. He replied, "No other colour exists beyond black".

TA, p. 711

23. Shaqiq Balkhi: "Poverty is accompanied by three things: a heart that is carefree, a conscience at ease, and a soul in peace."

TA, p. 237

24. Shaqiq Balkhi was asked, "How can it be known that a devotee prefers poverty to wealth?". He replied, "He is so afraid of becoming wealthy that he clutches onto poverty, just as previously he feared becoming poor, and tenaciously held onto wealth."

TS (S), p. 65

25. Shaqiq Balkhi: "Poverty is safeguarded by you seeing poverty as coming from Him, from God

to you, and your consequent indebtness in that you are not obliged to provide for anyone else, and the daily bread allocated to you does not decrease."

TS (S), p. 65

26. Abu Ḥafṣ Ḥaddâd: "Poverty is not complete until one likes giving more than getting."

TA, p. 461

27. Abu Ḥafṣ Naishaburi: "The true *faqir* is he who in every state is at the bidding of time *(waqt)*[1]. If some extraneous inspiration enters his heart which causes him to attend to himself and distracts him from time's behest, he is frightened and rejects it."

TS (S), p. 117

28. Abu Ḥafṣ Naishaburi: "The noblest poverty is before God; the most despicable towards material forms. The noblest self-sufficiency *(al-esteghnâ')* is the Divine; the basest independance that of vulgar people."

TS (S), p. 117

29. Abu Ḥafṣ Ḥaddâd: "The best way for a devotee to draw near to God is by constant spiritual poverty in every state, careful adherence to the tradition *(sunna)* of the Prophet in every action, and pursuit of a lawful livelihood."

RQ, p. 458

30 Yaḥyâ ebn Ma'adh: "Poverty is to fear it's

1. See chapter VI for a discussion of this concept.

departure. The sign of true poverty is that, though one has reached the perfection of saintship and contemplation and self-annihilation, one always dreads its decline and departure, until such a point of perfection is reached that seperation is no longer feared."

KM, p. 28-29

31. Yaḥyâ ebn Ma'âdh: "The reality of poverty is that one becomes rich through God alone; its outer guise is non-attention to ways and means."

RQ, p. 453

32. Ebrâhim Adham: "We sought poverty, and wealth appeared before us. People sought wealth, and poverty enveloped them."

RQ, p. 455

33. It is related that one day a man brought ten thousand dirhams to Ebrâhim Adham. He refused it, saying, "Do you wish to remove my name from the register of the spiritually poor by this sum?"

RQ, p. 453

34. Ebrâhim Khawâṣṣ "Poverty is a robe of honour, the cloak of apostles, and the mantle of the upright."

AM

35. Abu Torâb Nakhshabi: "The *faqir*'s food is whatever he finds, his clothes whatever covers him, and his home wherever he stops."

TS (S), p. 149

36. Abo'l-Faḍhl Ḥasan: "Reality consists in two things: First, integrity of one's spiritual poverty before God, which is among the principles of devotion. Second, the meticulous following of the example of the Prophet, which means the denial of all ease and advantage to oneself."

TA, p. 817

37. Shâh Kermâni: "Poverty has three signs. The first is that the worth of the world departs from your heart such that gold and silver are as dust to you; and whenever gold or silver falls into your hand, you shake it off, as you would dust. The second is that the sight of people no longer delights your heart. Their praise and blame is one to you; the former does not inflate you, nor the latter chasten you. The third is that indulgence in fleshly passions ceases to give you pleasure. As sensualists delight in satiation of their appetites and lusts, so you enjoy hunger, thirst and continence. When you gain these qualities, be assiduous in following the way of devotees, but if this is not your manner, why occupy yourself with these sayings?"

TA, p. 380

38. Abu 'Ali Rudbâri recounted that Abu Bakr Zaqqâq asked him, "When in need, why don't *faqirs* set aside adequate provision for themselves?"

I replied, "The Provider makes them needless of provision."

"So I thought," rejoined Abu Bakr Zaqqâq, "but a further meaning comes to me."

"Tell me", I said.

He replied, "Because they are a group whom possessions do not benefit. Their poverty is from

God, and having God, poverty cannot aggrieve them".

MH, p. 377

39. Shebli: "The *faqir* is one whom only God can make wealthy".

TA, p. 33

40. Shebli: "There are four hundred spiritual degrees common to the darvish. The least degree would be for a darvish to possess the entire world, then to give it away as alms, then to think, 'Ah! If only I had stored away a day's sustenance!' — even then, his poverty would be false."

TA, p. 633

41. Sahl ebn 'Abdo'llâh: "No denser veil than pretension exists between God and the devotee. There is no closer way to God than spiritual impoverishment before God."

TA, p. 315

42. Sahl ebn 'Abdo'llâh was asked: "When may a *faqir* rest?" He answered, "When he sees himself as living only in the time (*waqt*) in which he is."

RQ, p. 462

43. Sahl ebn 'Abdo'llâh was asked, "Who is a true *faqir?*" He replied, "One who doesn't beg, doesn't refuse what he is offered, and doesn't store away his wealth."

AM

44. According to Shaikh Abu 'Ali Fârmadi'[1], Râbe'a crawled on her side for seven years until she reached Mt. 'Arefât. There an invisible Voice called out, rebuking her: "You imposter, what is this 'quest' you are occupied with? If you desire Me, then I will show you one flash of My Glory and consume you".

Râbe'a begged, "O Lord of Majesty, Râbe'a lacks such a capacity. I yearn simply for a taste of spiritual poverty *(faqr)*".

The Voice replied, "O Râbe'a, poverty is the scourge of our wrath, which we have laid on the way of the saints. When less than a hair's breadth remains between them and Our Vision, We turn their affairs upside down, and cast them into grief. Yet you still are enthralled by the seventy thousand veils of your own day and age. Only when you emerge from behind these veils and step firmly upon the Way will you be worthy to profess Our poverty."

TA, p. 75-76

45. People asked Ebn Jalâ', "When does a man merit the name of poverty?" He replied, "Poverty ascribed to a *faqir* by his own assertion is false. Rather, the poverty of a true *faqir* is devoid of all pretense and self-advantage."

RQ, p. 457

46. Ebn Jalâ': "Poverty is owning nothing, and whatever is in your hands, not considering it your own until you give it away."

AM

1. Abu 'Ali Fadhl ebn Moḥammad Fârmadi was a Sufi master who was born in the village of Farmad, a suburb of Tus in 1011. Shah Ne'mato'llâh's master: Shaikh Yâfe'i, in his *Obituaries (motawâfiât)* mentions his death date as 1084.

47. When asked about poverty, Ebn Jalâ'
remained silent. Then he stepped outside for a moment and came back. "What happened?" they asked. "I had four silver *dangs,* and was ashamed to mention poverty until I had given them away".

TA, p. 498

48. Morta'esh: "The aspiration of a *faqir* should not outstep his stride."

RQ, p. 458

49. Nuri: " *'Faqirs'* are characterised by tranquility in not having, and charity in having."

AM

50. Asked of the true *faqir,* Nuri replied: "Someone who does not refer to God through secondary causes, and maintains his peace whatever his state."

TS(S), p. 169

51. Somnun Moḥebb: "The *faqir* is one who loves poverty as the ignorant person loves money. He is as terrified of money as the ignorant person is of poverty."

TA, p. 514

52. 'Abdo'llâh Manâzel: "Poverty which isn't compulsory has no virtue."

TA, p. 541

53. 'Abdo'llâh Manâzel: "Poverty is to divorce this world and the next, and to become wealthy through the Lord of both worlds."

TA, p. 541

54. 'Ali Sahl Eṣfahâni: "I begged for power and found it in knowledge. I begged for honor and found it in poverty. I begged for health and found it in asceticism. I begged my account be lessened before God and found it in silence. I begged for consolation and found it in despair."

TA, p. 544

55. Abo'l-Ḥasan Mozaiyen: "There were more ways to God than the stars in heaven. Now no way remains but poverty, which is the most authentic of all ways."

RQ, p. 459

56. Abo'l-Ḥasan Mozaiyen: "Whoever becomes impoverished before God, and perfects himself in poverty by observing the manners of poverty, God will grant him through poverty independence from all else but Him."

TS, p. 384

57. Abo'l-Ḥasan Mozaiyen: "The sincere *faqir* finds consolation in what God apportions for him, and is disquieted by the liberality of all others — from whatever direction it may come."

TS, p. 385

58. Mozaffer Kermânshâhi was asked, "Who is

a *faqir?*" He replied, "Someone from whom no-one needs anything." Ansâri comments, "No one needs anything from him because he is, in fact, the Needed One (*Ḥâjat)*"

TS(A), p. 411

59. Moẓaffer Kermânshâhi: "The *faqir* is one who has no need of God."

RQ, p. 461

60. Abu Bakr Ṭâher 'Abhari: "The *faqir's* practice is having no desires. Should he possess a desire, however, it must not exceed his need."

TS (S), p. 394;

61. Abu Bakr Abi Sa'dân: "The *faqir* is one who lacks wherewithal[1]. This privation makes requisite the application of the term poverty *(faqr)* to him, and facilities his way to the Causer."

TS(S), p. 422

62. Abu Bakr Meṣri: "The sincere *faqir* owns nothing and is owned by no one."

RQ, p. 463

63. Once Abu Bakr Warraq exclaimed: "O how happy is the *faqir* in this world and the next!"

Begged to elucidate, he replied, "The princes of this world do not levy taxes on him, and in the next,

1. *asbâb:* literally means 'effects' 'causes' and here implies efficient causes, or the natural agents of phenomena (as well as the economic meaning 'means', 'conveniences') *vis-à-vis* the Causer *(mosabbib)* or the *sui causa* which is God.

 God will not call him to account."

RQ, p. 466

64. Abu Bakr Wâseti related: "For quite a while I was puzzled as to why the Sufis had chosen poverty over everything else. No one gave me a satisfactory answer until I asked Naṣr 'ebn Ḥammâmi. He replied, "Because poverty is the first of the stations of Divine Unity *(tauḥid)*". His answer made me content.

AM

65. Abu Bakr Kattâni: "When poverty in relation to God is complete, then wealth in God is complete, for neither of these states are complete without the other."

AM

66. Abu Bakr Moḥammad ebn Dâwud Daqqi: "The *faqir* is one who outwardly owns no possessions, and inwardly has no inclination towards any."

TS (S), p. 449

67. Daqqi was asked why *foqarâ* in their mystical states show such scant courtesy towards the Divine. "It is because," he answered, "of their descent from the Reality to the exteriority of knowledge."

TS (S), p. 449

68. Daqqi was asked, "What is the difference

between Poverty and Sufism?" He replied, "Poverty is one of the states of Sufism."

TS (S), p. 448

69. Sirwâni: "The *faqir* is the child of his own moment *(waqt)*[1]. Whenever he becomes aware of another moment, he deserts poverty."

TS (A), p. 484

70. Ḥallâj: "The *faqir* has no need of that which is other than God and sees through God."

TA, p. 588

71. Masuḥi: "The *faqir* is one who has realised detachment from all material means."

RQ, p. 462

72. Masuḥi: "The *faqir* is one whom gratuities do not make wealthy, nor afflictions impoverish."

AM

73. Fâres related: "Once I met a *faqir* on whom the effects of hunger and want were manifest. I asked him why he did not try to provide for himself by begging. He replied: "I am frightened lest people refuse my solicitation and hence fail to reach salvation.""

AM

1. *Waqt* also means time, or instant (of non-temporal ecstatic realisation). Here the implication is that poverty is a state (c f. no. 68) which overcomes the mystic through the grace of the Eternal Now. See Chap. VI: 'Metaphysical Time', for further explanation.

74. Moḥammad ebn Abe'l-Ward: "One of the rules of spiritual poverty observed by *faqirs* is to refrain from blame or criticism of those enmeshed in worldly ambition, and, instead they are merciful and charitably disposed towards them and pray for them, until God relieves them of this affliction."

TS (S), p. 251

75. Abu 'Abdo'llâh Maqarri: "The sincere *faqir* possesses all things but is possessed by nothing."

TS (S), p. 245

76. Abu 'Abdo'llâh Maghrebi: "The contented *faqirs* are Gods' trustees on earth, a visible demonstration of God to His devotees. God, through their presence prevents calamities from afflicting humankind."

TS (S), p. 245

77. 'Abu 'Abdo'llâh Maghrebi: "The basest of all people is the *faqir* who acts obsequiously before the wealthy, and the noblest of all people is a wealthy person who renders homage to and venerates the *faqir*."

TS (S), p. 244

78. Yusef ebn Ḥosain Râzi: "The *faqir* is one who safeguards his 'moment', so if another moment enters his awareness while he his engaged in his 'moment' he becomes unworthy of the name of poverty."

TS (S), p. 188

79. Abu Moḥammad Jorairi: "The *faqir* does not seek the favour of the world unless he fears the

estrangement from it will make him unable to fulfill his spiritual duties."

ST, p. 280

80. Abu Moḥammad Jorairi: "Poverty's ethic requires that one should not seek the non-existent until the existent vanishes."

Kalâbâdhi comments, "He means that one should seek no further as long as anything of the world is present before him. When what he has is gone, then he pursues only what is necessary to support himself [financially and psychologically] or to fulfill his spiritual duties."

KST, p. 280

81. Moḥammad ebn Faḍhl Balkhi: "Concord *(mowâfeqat)* is the basis of love; abandonment of repose is the basis of union; realisation of one's faults is the basis of poverty and poverty is the basis of devotion to the Truth."

TS (S), p. 216

82. Abu Ḥamzâ Baghdâdi: "It is difficult to love poverty. Only the sincere have the patience to maintain it."

TS (S), p. 298

83. Bâbâ Ṭâher: "Poverty is a sea of affliction, knowledge its ship, and *wajd*[1] it's waves. When the

1. "In the terminology of Sufism, *wajd* is that which, when it reaches the heart causes the sufi to become aware of fear or sadness; it is the unveiling of something from the unseen world." — from the author's *In the Tavern of Ruin*, Chap. IV, (N.Y. 1978), p. 50.

 waves swell, the ship flounders."

TS (S), p. 298

84. Bâbâ Ṭâher: "The genuine *faqir* partakes of all the characteristics and attributes of God but one, which is 'The Rich' *('al-Ghâni),* for he is poor. With all other Divine Names, he is unified."

TKQ, p. 575

85. Bâbâ Ṭâher: "There are three aspects to the practice of poverty: One which leads to the aquisition of an outer poverty, a second which leads to the acquisition of an inner poverty, and a third derivative from the inner poverty.

The first brings one reward in the hereafter. The second brings about return to Reality. The third detaches one from all but God."

TKQ, p. 580

86. Bâbâ Ṭâher: "Poverty is severence of attachment to secondary causes *(asbâb)*".

TKQ, p. 581

87. Bâbâ Ṭâher: "The true *faqir* knows himself to be propertyless *vis-à-vis* the Divine Lordship, while the reality of Lordship never deserts his innermost consciousness."

TKQ, p. 584

88. Darrâj: "While rummaging through my master's satchel, searching for his eye-salve, I happened to discover some money. I was astounded. I turned to him and said, 'I found some money in your satchel!'

" 'So I see,' he replied, 'here, hand it to me. Now take it and purchase something.'

"I protested, 'Tell me, in God's Name, what is the secret behind this money?'.

' "God has given me in this world', he replied, 'only this much of his yellow and white (gold and silver). I wanted to will it to be wound in my winding sheet and thus be reassigned to God." '

AM

89. "It has been said that whoever desires poverty for its honour dies impoverished, but whoever desires poverty in order to be engaged exclusively with God, dies wealthy *(ghani)*[1]."

RQ, p. 549

90. "It has been said that the light of the *faqir* is in three things: vigilance over the innermost consciousness *(serr)* fulfillment of religious obligations, and maintenance of spiritual poverty."

RQ, p. 454

91. "It has been said that the reality of poverty is that the *faqir* only be made wealthy by poverty."

RQ, p. 457

92. 'Abdo'l-Qâder Gilâni: "A *faqir* patient before God is better than a rich person grateful to God, and a *faqir* grateful to God excells both the former, but best of all is the *faqir* who is patient and grateful."

Jomhurat al-auliyâ'

1. The root of the Arabic term for 'rich' and 'wealthy': *ghani*, may also connote the ability 'to go without' or 'to have no need of'. Its implication in this context is spiritual self-sufficiency.

93. "One day while listening to a mystical concert *(samâ)* in the company of Maulânâ Rumi[1], a sufi fell to meditating on the significance of poverty. As the concert continued, Rumi sang this *robâ'i*:

Poverty is the substance;
All else accident.
Poverty is the remedy,
Everything else a malady.

The world is a lie,
All pride, all vanity;
Poverty is a mystery
And *raison d'être* of the world.

NO, p. 462

94. "Abu 'Abdo'llâh Raḍhi related, 'I went to visit Walid Saqqâ', intending to ask him of poverty. He raised his head and said: The name of poverty pertains only to someone who has thought solely of God and never anything else throughout his whole lifetime, and on the Day of Judgement can justify this claim.' "

NO, p. 37

95. Abo'l-Nahâwandi: "The culmination of poverty is the beginning of Sufism."

MH, p. 118

96. Abu Bakr Warrâq: "Men are of three kinds: rulers, scholars, and *foqarâ*. When rulers become

1. The famous classical Persian poet and saint: Jalâlod-din Rumi (d. 1273).

corrupt, the welfare and prosperity of the peasants go to ruin. When the scholars become corrupt, obedience and the observance of the religious law *(shari'at)* declines. When the *foqarâ* are corrupted however, human nature itself becomes decadent. The degeneration of rulers lies in injustice and oppression *(ẓolm)*; that of the scholars arises from greed, and that of the *foqarâ* derives from hypocrisy."

NO, p. 125

97. Ruzbehân Baqli describes "the ascension to the station of poverty" in the following colloquy between lover and Beloved:

> One day, in the ṣolitude of the soul, I heard the thundering of the kettledrum of Pre-Eternity. I saw the bride-to-be of the Uncreated One. Love stirred me to prostrate myself before Her loveliness.
>
> "O dualist!" she chided me, "turn away from the province of Uncreated Being! — for the sun-disc of the Sphere of Pre-Eternity will not be dimmed by a cloud of created being."
>
> "What is the aim of *Tauḥid?*"[1] I queried.
>
> "Poverty ('deprivation', *faqr)* of *Tauḥid.*"
>
> "What is the ultimate meaning of poverty?" I asked.
>
> "Shame-facedness in this world and the next," She cited.[2]

1. *Tauḥid* is the monotheistic Oneness of God. See the author's *Sufism: Meaning, Knowledge and Unity* (New York, 1981).
2. This is a Tradition *(ḥadith)* ascribed to the Prophet. See the author's *Traditions of the Prophet,* Vol. II, p. 39 for fuller commentary on this saying.

"One may gather an indication of this here," I commented, "but who can endure such shame in the hereafter?"

"Truly you are not dedicated to poverty," She pronounced, "unless you are disgraced in this world and the next."

SS, p. 334

98. Hojwiri: "The *faqir* is not simply one whose hand is empty of provisions, but one whose inner nature is void of desires. For example, if God gives one money and one desires to keep it, then one is no *faqir,* while if one chooses to renounce the gift, one is still no *faqir,* for both desires are conditioned by ones own initiative, and poverty is the abandonment of initiative."

KM, (trans.), p. 25

99. Aḥmad ebn 'Aṣem Anṭâki: "The most beneficial poverty is that which you regard as honorable, and with which you are well pleased." Hojwiri comments: "The honour of the vulgar consists in affirmation of secondary causes, but the honour of the *faqir* consists in denying secondary causes and in affirming the Causer, and in referring everything to Him, and in being well pleased with His decrees. Poverty is the non-existence of secondary causes. Poverty detached from a secondary cause is with God, and wealth attached to a secondary cause is with itself. Therefore, secondary causes involve the state of being veiled [from God], while their absence involves the state of unveiledness. Whatever beauty exists on earth and in heaven comes from contentment with the Divine Will and unveilment,

whereas being veiled from God is to be discontented."

KM, (trans., slightly modified), p. 127

100. Manṣur ebn 'Ammâr: "There are two classes of men: those who have need of God — they hold the highest rank from the standpoint of the sacred law — and those who pay no regard to their need of God, because they know that God has provided for their creation and livelihood and death and life and happiness and misery. They need God alone, and having Him, are independant of all else." Hojwiri comments: "The former, through seeing their need, are veiled from seeing the Divine providence, whereas the latter, in not seeing their own need, are unveiled and independent. The former enjoy felicity, but the latter enjoy the Giver of felicity."

KM, (trans.), p. 127

Poverty According to Anṣâri

On the *via paupertatis*
the eyes of the senses'
sight are all illusion
and the ears are closed
to all but the pauper's tales.

Be rubble, trodden
in the dust of His footpath
for princes of the world
lay poverty's dust as balm
upon their eyelids.

TfA, II, p. 662

From *One Hundred Battlefields*[1]

From the Battlefield of Remembrance of God *(dhekhn)* arises the Battlefield of Poverty. God declares: "O humanity! You are poor in relation to God." (XXXV:15)

Poverty is darvish-hood and is of three types:

1. Compulsory poverty.
2. Voluntary poverty.
3. Realised poverty.

Compulsory poverty is tripartite: expiation; chastisement; severance.

The condition of expiation is indicated by expectation and waiting; the state of chastisement is indicated by stricture and anguish, and the state of severance by dissatisfaction and complaining, as for example, where the *Qoran* describes the hypocrites *(monâfeqin)*: "...and if they are not given alms, they are enraged." (IV:58)

Voluntary poverty is also tripartite: elevation, proximity to God, magnanimity.

Elevation is reached by contentment *(qanâ'at)*, proximity to God by means of resignation *(redha)*, and magnanimity by means of selflessness *('ithar)*.

Realised poverty is tripartite as well: [Perceiving] no oppression on God's part nor any sinlessness on the servants part: perceiving the infinitude of the Divine Bounty and feeling helpless in numbering the praises due to God. God declares: "Those whom God wills to afflict, you (Mohammad) are not in a positon to assist them in the face of His will, for God does not wish to purify their hearts." (V: 41)

1. This work by Anṣâri comprises one hundred battlefields *(ṣad maidân)* or arenas of spiritual combat, a masterpiece of metaphysical and moral insights composed in rhyming prose. SM, p. 68

From *Pilgrims Waystations:*[1]

God declares: "O humanity! You are poor in relation to God." Poverty is freedom from coveting possessions. It comprises three degrees:

1. Ascetic Poverty. This implies renunciation of the world's wealth, both in the pursuit and the retention of it, and maintaining silence concerning it, offering neither praise nor censure; and absolute detachment from the world, neither following nor shunning it. This is the 'noble poverty' so often lauded.

2. Return to the Divine Source by contemplation of God's graces. Attaining to this degree, one gains liberation from selfhood in one's actions; ones' mystical states become empty of egoism, and one's contemplation of spiritual stations becomes purified of all turbidity.

3. The Perfection of Needfulness *(eḍhterâr)*[2]. At this degree the devotee is diffused (*taqatto'*) into the Divine Unity, becomes detached from himself and is constrained by the bonds of contemplation. This is the Sufi's poverty.

MS, p. 121

The two types of Poverty

There are two types of poverty:

1. The poverty of created beings.
2. Poverty as a quality in relation to God.

The poverty of created beings is of a general nature and comprehends all temporal occurrences

1. The *Manâzel as-sâ'erin* by Anṣâri, concerns the stages of purgation of the heart, upon which over seven major commentaries by major Sufi masters have been composed.
2. *Eḍhterâr* has a twofold significance: (a) utter indigence on the devotees part in relation to God, and (b) Gods overwhelming compulsion, rendering this degree of poverty particularly subtle.

which have come into being from nothingness. "O humanity! You are poor in relation to God." (XXXV: 15) Every creature has need of its Creator. Poverty signifies need; a need initially for creation, and ultimately for sustenance. God however is without need, while all need Him.

Concerning poverty as a quality relative to God, in a eulogy of the Prophet's Companions, God mentions "those *foqarâ* who are refugees" (LIX: 8). The epithet 'poor' was employed to conceal their wealth, lest anyone recognise them.

TfA, II, p. 285

Poverty's Graduations

According to the gnostics, poverty has three graduations:

1. Want *(ḥâjat)*
2. Poverty *(faqr)*
3. Destitution *(maskanat)*

One who feels 'want' is subservient to the world in as much as it blocks his realisation of true poverty. One endowed with 'poverty', however, while not attached to the world, inclines towards the hereafter and is consoled by paradisical bounties. One graced with 'destitution', on the other hand, desires only God, not being moved by heaven's bounties and graces. His sole attraction is to the mystery of the Bountiful.

TfA, I, p. 404

The *Faqir's* Requiem

The prerequisite of Love is jealousy,[1] and God's

1. In the sense that the Beloved demands the exclusive attention of the lover.

friends do not divulge their mystical states to the vulgar. The *faqir* is one who has no care for this world or the next, being constantly in contemplation of God. Enriched by God, he is poor *(darvish)* in all things.

Power must lie within the human breast, not within a treasure chest. In heaven and earth, the *faqir* has no handhold other than God. He has no concern for himself and has already chanted a funeral requiem over all that pertains to his 'essence' and his 'personality'.

TfA, II, p. 286

Abo'l-Mofâkher Yaḥyâ Bâkhzari on Poverty

The degrees of poverty are two: a complete poverty and a consummate poverty.

Complete poverty signifies the purgation of the *faqir's* reality *(ḥaqiqat)* of all things, all imposed limitations. It is his self-obliteration in the knowledge of God, so only his natural predisposition *(este'dâd)* and the seeking implanted in his essence *(ṭalab-e dhâti)*[1] remain. In this regard, the *faqir* needs all things, while nothing needs him, for 'predisposition dictates need'.[2] The *faqir*'s predisposition, the seeking implanted in his essence, longs for the imprint of being, and consequently he is dependent on all beings. Hence the saying: 'poverty is a need pertaining to the essence, to which need is inherent, just as the Rich *(al-Ghani)* is necessarily independant of need.'

Vis-á-vis this 'complete' poverty is the plane of the Rich, in need of nothing, and all in need of Him.'

However, consummate poverty signifies pur-

[1] The innate quest within every part to attain the whole. (Author's note)
[2] An Arabic saying

 gation of the *faqir's* reality of all things, all imposed limitations, including his natural predisposition and the seeking implanted in his essence. He is effaced in God's knowledge, and qualities of character can no longer be attributed to him. Being emptied of his predisposition and the seeking implanted in his essence, the *faqir* on this level, needs nothing. Nothing is left of himself, neither apprehension nor feeling for anything. This state occurs at the station of 'relegation of the trust[1] of existential egohood back to it's 'Owner' — the Reality, the Transcendent; as God says: "God commands that you return that with which you have been entrusted." (IV: 58)

AA, p.35

Moḥammad Ghazâli on Poverty

By definition, poverty is the privation of what is essentially needed by a human being. If these human essentials are present, however, and the person is fully able to fend for himself, such a person is not termed a *faqir*. Likewise, privation of what is unessential to a person, is not called poverty. Once this is understood, there is no doubt that all beings other than God are poor *(faqir)*, since the perpetuation of their beings in the immediate moment is constantly dependent on God's grace. Were a being to exist with no other origin than itself, it would be the Absolute Independent.[2] Because it is unimaginable to think that more than one being of this nature exists, it must follow that only one being exists, upon which all else are

[1] According to the *Qoran* (II, 30) man is designated as the viceroy of God on earth, which by extension, indicates the commitment of the ego to God.
[2] al-Ghani, 'The Rich'

dependent. All beings are sustained and succoured by this Being. This is the implication of God's word: "and God is Rich, and you are poor." (XLVII:36) This is the significance of poverty in an absolute sense.

EO, p. 519

'Ezzo'd-Din Maḥmud Kâshâni on Poverty

The wayfarer to Reality only reaches the station of poverty (the non-possession of means of livelihood: *asbâb*) after attaining to the station of asceticism *(zohd)*; for only after his fondness for the world has disappeared does his non-possession become true renunciation.

Poverty is characterized successively by a name, a practice, and a reality. It's name is non-possession, though with a tendency still towards possession. It's practice is non-possession achieved through asceticism. Its reality comes in realisation of the impossibility of all ownership. This is because those intimate with poverty's reality perceive everything as being in God's omnipotent control. No one else can, thus, be attributed as having real ownership. Poverty is rooted in the essence of the being of the achiever thereof; neither presence nor absence of things can affect such a one. Even if the entire world should chance to come under his control, he would care nothing for its possession. One concerned with only the formal practice of poverty, however, merely possesses poverty in a transient sense. For such a one, the reality of poverty remains inwardly unrealised, for it's meaning is as yet ungrounded in his essence. As long as one considers oneself an 'owner', the absence of things stirs one to anxiety. This category of *faqir,* while relying on the virtues of spiritual poverty to the extent of seeking recompense in the hereafter, inclines towards abnegation of the externals of wealth and ownership, even more so than the wealthy flee from the externals of poverty.

Concerning the superiority of poverty to wealth and vice-versa, Sufis have offered different points of view. The correct doctrine, however, is that while poverty supercedes the virtues of wealth for novices and aspirants as they approach the mid-point of the Way, they are of equal status for adepts towards the end of the Path. At this level the presence or absence of outer riches and possessions has no effect on the reality and essence of poverty with which an adept is inwardly graced.

MH, p. 375-6

درويش و درويشی

II

The Darvish

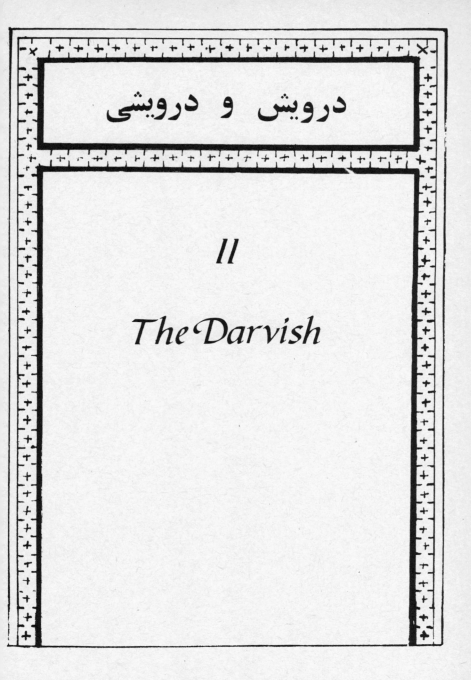

The Darvish

The bowers of eternity are the asylum of darvishes
The source of all pre-eminence
lies in service to the darvishes .

Ḥâfeẓ

Darvish: Its Etymological Origin

By definition, the word 'darvish' signifies a beggar, or mendicant, asking for alms from door to door. "The original word was *'darwiz'* (درویز) the *za* (زاء) is said to have been altered in Persian usage to *sh* (ش) at a later date. In this respect, *darwiz* is supposed originally to have been *darâwiz* (درا ویز) literally: 'one who hangs onto a door,' and since beggars petitioning for alms seized the door-rings of houses, beggars were termed *darwishes.*

Other philologists trace the etymology of darvish from *dariwiz* (دریوز) theorizing that *yâ* (یا) and *vav* (واو) were transposed, and that the Persian *sh* (ش) eventually replaced the final ending *zâ,* (زاء), while noting that the compound *yuz* (یوز) is the imperative form of *yuzidan* (یوزیدن), meaning 'to seek'.

If the term *darwish,* pronounced *'darvish'* in modern Persian, is employed to mean spiritual poverty and need for God, it is synonymous with the terms *sufi* and *faqir,* and hence, in translating Arabic mystical texts into Persian, the Arabic *faqir* is rendered by the Persian *darwish.* Some scholars, attempting to preserve both it's mystical and worldly meanings (i.e. of spiritual poverty and material mendicancy) employ a further compound: *dorwish* (دُرّویش) to denote a *faqir* who is a mystic. This word is composed of *dorr,* which means 'pearl' in Arabic and — *rish* (ریش) a suffix derived from the Persian comparative ending — *wash*(وَش), meaning 'like' or 'by', thus their term literally meaning 'a pearl-like (mystic)',"

—*Ghiyâth al-loghat*

Apropos of the above discussion, a distinction prevalent amongst Naqshbandi and Qâderi *foqarâ* in Kurdistan in western Iran, should be mentioned. Naqshbandi *foqarâ,* who are usually strict Muslims and rigid adherents to the canon law, are generally called 'sufis'. *Foqarâ* of the Qâderi order, on the other hand, generally poor in their material circumstances, and more oriented towards spiritual intoxication, ecstasy, and musical audition *(sama),* are usually referred to as 'darvishes'.

Sayings of the Masters
Concerning the Term 'Darvish'

The radiant beam which shines
transmuting to gold
the black heart

Is the alchemy discovered
in the company
of the darvishes.

Ḥâfeẓ

1. Yusef ebn Ḥosain: Just as the greedy person is the worst of human beings, so the sincere darvish is the noblest.

TA, p. 389

2. Abu 'Abdo'llâh Maghrebi: The darvish who abstains from the world, while engaging in no virtuous deeds, is still a grain more worthy and virtuous than the devout theologian.

TA, p. 56

3. Abo'l-Ḥasan Kharaqâni: The darvish is someone without a 'here' or a 'hereafter', feeling no fondness for either heaven or earth, because relative to the heart, both are contemptible.

TA, p. 695

4. Abo'l-Ḥasan Kharaqani: The darvish is someone whose heart is emptied of thoughts. He talks without speaking; he sees and hears, yet has neither sight nor hearing; he eats but tastes nothing. He has neither motion nor rest, neither joy nor grief.

TA, p. 701

5. Abu Bakr Waseṭi: The darvish should proceed by the light of the heart, yet the mystics of our day all walk with canes.

TA, p. 701

6. Ja'far Kholdi: When you find a darvish who

 eats excessively know that one of three things is present within him: either that he has been unconscious of a mystical moment *(waqt)* confered upon him, or that subsequently he will go astray, or that his spiritual state has been aborted.

TA, p. 753

7. Yaḥyâ ebn Ma'âdh was asked, "What does it mean to be a darvish?" He replied, "To be rich in the world solely through God's wealth."

TA, p. 372

8. When Abu Ḥafṣ Ḥaddâd was asked what it means to be a darvish, he replied "To show oneself abject *(shekastegi)* before the Almighty".

TA, p. 398

9. Anṣâri: " 'What is being a darvish?' 'It is an unpainted exterior, and an interior without strife. The darvish has no name or reputation, and knows neither war nor peace.' "

RA

10. Abu Moḥammad Jorairi: Being a darvish is 'not having', but what you do have, not considering your own. In this light, the Qoran refers to, "those who prefer to nurse fugitives before caring for themselves, even though poverty become their lot." (LIX:9), meaning that one should not look for success from patience.[1]

ST, p. 280

1. According to an Arabic proverb, 'The key to success (*faraj*, 'opening') is patience.' Here, Jorairi emphasizes the virtue of patience, independent of any fruit it may bear.

11. In eulogy of the darvishes[1] Ansâri writes: There exists a group whose robes have never snarled on Envy's briars, whose piety and purity has never been overcast by stormclouds in the wasteland of Egocentric Desire, nor their eyes ever bleared by any mist from the abyss of Sensual Passion.

They are princes of the Path, attired in darvish rags, angelic temperments incarnate in human forms, pilgrims sojourning to Reality, joyously striding the road to their own annihilation.

TfA, II, p. 517

12. Sa'di: The darvish's appearance is a tattered robe and disheveled hair but his reality is a living heart and a mortified soul.

G, p. 231

13. Abu Bakr Hamadâni: There are three qualities to becoming a darvish: one, not coveting anything; two, not declining what you are offered; and three, not hoarding what you receive.

TS (A), p. 434

14. Abu Sa'id Abe'l-Khair: Darvishes are not those who claim the name only. Those who make claims are not darvishes. The word *'darvish'* signifies the qualities of actually being a darvish. Anyone in search of the Truth, must of necessity encounter darvishes on his way, as they are the doorway to Reality.

AT, p. 307

1. This passage is written in commentary on Surah LIX: 9, as in no. 10 above.

15. Commending the darvishes, Ḥâj Mollâ Hâdi Sabzewâri writes:

All the world's coinage, all its mint and print
is false, counterfeit;
the true coin alone
is the alchemy in the glance
of a perfect darvish.
Fire doesn't pertain to what ignited
some burning bush in Palestine.
The ardour in the darvishes' heart
is the true fire.

Ritual prayers, puritan zeal fail to succeed.
Love alone works, love alone lasts,
love alone is the flower of the darvishes.

Diwan

16. In a section of the *Mathnawi,* Rumi speaks of the darvishes:

God guides the affairs of the darvish athirst for God, while one athirst for what is other than God is diverted in aspiration towards ungodly things; such a one goes astray in ignorance and perversion. He is but the image of a darvish; he is not of the soul's family. Do not toss a bone to the portrait of a dog! Poverty he does possess, for sure, poverty for food, not poverty for the Truth. Place your platters less before these lifeless images of men. The bread-darvish is but a land-fish, a mere fish-shape which has fled the sea. Just a household bird, not a celestial *Simurgh;* preoccupied with his stomach, not occupied with God. For the sake of a morsel he may love God, but he is not in the soul a lover of the Beautiful and the Sublime.

MM, I: vv. 2752-56

17. And again, Rumi writes: "No darvish exists in the world or, if he exists, is not a darvish. His essence, indeed, subsists in Divinity for all eternity, but his personality has perished in the Ipseity of the Almighty. Like a candle's flame in the presence of the sun, it exists, but by all formal reckoning, it is not. It exists in essence, in that it burns cotton on contact, but in the glare of the sun it is not. The candle exists but without giving light, for it is annihilated in the sunlight."

MM, III: 3669-73

18. "How is it," Abu Sa'id was asked, "that God can be seen, yet not the darvish?" He answered, "It is because God exists, and existence can be seen. The darvish, however, does not exist, and non-existence is invisible."

AT, p. 313

19. The following three *roba'i* are ascribed to Abu Sa'id Abe'l-Khair:

Will nothing; strive not to prevail
over this or that,
Unswayed by either woe or grief
if you're a darvish.

In Divinity's dominion, alone
rejoice in one thing:
Detachment from everything
be it celestial or terrestrial

All that exists, exists for darvishes.
They are antecedent to everyone,
foremost in God's court.

Accompany them; befriend them, they are
alchemy,
able to change your being's copper to gold.

Look not for profit
Think not of loss
among the darvishes:
Nor figure you possess
Even a strand of hair
of self-volition;
Nor call a mystic
One whom faith obsesses
yet pursues the world.

AT

20. In a few lines, Rumi defines the actuality of 'the darvish':

'The darvish' is one who in each out-breathing
gives free away a whole universe,
who cries forth the secrets of every world.

'The darvish' begs for no mans bread,
'the darvish' is the quickener of the soul.

21. Kharaqâni was asked, "What does it mean to be a darvish?" He replied, "It is an ocean fed by three tributaries: abstinence, generosity and independence of God's creatures."

NrO, p. 110

22. Anṣâri: "To be a darvish means to be a lump of sifted earth with a little water sprinkled on top, neither hurting the soles of the feet, nor scattering a trail of dust behind."[1]

RA, p. 35

Tales of The Darvishes

1. Sa'di: A band of ruffians and rogues fell out with a darvish, insulting him, then striking and wounding him. The darvish went to the master of his order, complaining about the mishap. His master answered, "The mantle of the darvishes, my son, is the garment of resignation *(reḍha)*. Whoever wears their costume, yet cannot tolerate having his desires frustrated, is merely a pretender, and their mantle is forbidden to him.

Small stones cannot darken
 the vast seething sea;
The gnostic affronted, offended by something,
 is only a shallow brook.

G, p. 222

2. Khair Nassâj: Once, when I entered a mosque a darvish accosted me, "O Master, grant me your charity, misfortune has befallen me." "What is that?" I asked. "I have been deprived of affliction and endowed with prosperity," he replied. So I glanced at him, and observed him to have acquired one dinar in alms.

TA, p. 546

1. See also the *Intimate Conversations (Monâjât)* of Anṣâri, tr. by W.M. Thackston (London, 1978), p. 216 for a slightly different rendition of this saying.

3. Hojwiri: Once a darvish encountered a king who enjoined him, “Ask a boon of me”. The darvish countered, “I will not ask a boon from one of my slaves.”

“How is that?” demanded the king. The darvish replied, “I have two slaves who are your masters: greed and covetousness.”

KM (trans., slightly modified), p. 20

صوفی و تصوف

III

The Sufi

Definitions of 'Sufism' and 'Sufi'.

A sufi in name,
in heart fault-free,
darvish and destitute
but joyous, ecstatic...

Ferdausi

Want nothing for yourself,
whether of heaven or earth,
want only the Beloved
if you're 'sufi'... 'pure souled'

Sanâ'i

In a previous book,[1] we mentioned a series of definitions of 'Sufism' and 'Sufi', given by great Masters of the Path. A further selection is presented below.

1. It is related that someone saw Bayazid in a dream, and asked him, "What is Sufism?" He replied, "To shut the door of comfort to oneself and to be seated behind the knee of suffering."

TA, p. 210

1. *Sufism: Meaning, Knowledge, and Unity*. (New York, 1981) pp.16-41

2. Sahl ebn ‘Abdo’llâh: Our faith is founded on three practices: emulating the conduct and character of the Prophet, consumption of only lawful food, and honesty in all one’s dealings.

TA, p. 315

3. Abu Sa‘id Kharrâz, when asked, “What is Sufism?” replied, “Submission to time *(waqt).*”

TA, p. 462

4. Shâh Ne‘mato’llâh: “Sufism is to qualify oneself with the qualities of God.”

RSh, IV, p. 157

5. Yusef ebn Ḥosain: “There is a select band among every nation appointed to be God’s stewards, whom God conceals from the sight of the vulgar. Within this nation, if such a company exists, they are the Sufis.”

TA, p. 387

6. Ebn Jalâ’: “The Sufi is a faqir detached from all intermediary causes.”

TA, p. 498

7. Abu ‘Abdo’llâh Torughadi: “The Sufi is concerned with God, the ascetic with his own soul.”

TA, p. 557

8. Kharaqâni: “Ninety-nine worlds lie at the Sufi’s disposal, one of which extends from earth

to heaven and encompasses the whole of the East and West, whereas in the other ninety-eight neither utterance nor vision are to be found."

TA, p. 700

9. Abo'l-Qâsem Naṣrâbâdi: "Sufism is a light from God pointing unto God, and a passing thought from God showing the way to God."

TA, p. 793

10. Abu Bakr ebn Abi-Sa'dân: "The Sufi transcends all qualities and is alien to all human convention, whereas the *faqir* is someone who lacks material means: this deprivation causes him to be graced with the name of poverty, and facilitates his way to the Causer of causes."

TS (A), p. 333

11. "When Moẓaffar Kermânshâhi was asked about Sufism he declared, 'It is a praiseworthy character.' "

TS (A), p. 411

12. Anṣâri: "Once a rogue[1] said to a Sufi, "The difference between us and you is that whatever we profess, we practice, whereas whatever you think, and whatever passes through your heart, you do."

TS (A)

1. A type of chivalrous ruffian who, though lacking a spiritual discipline nevertheless has some staunch ethical beliefs.

13. Shaikh Abo'l-Qâsem Maqarri Râzi: "Sufism is to maintain continuity in one's mystical states with God."

TS (A), p. 477

14. Abo'l-Ḥasan Sirwâni: "The Sufi is one who is familiar with the inspirations of the heart *(wâredât-e qalbi),* rather than one who engages in vocative remembrance *('aurâd).*"

TS (A), p. 263

15. Sirwâni: "The Sufi is one who has perfectly comprehended and progressed beyond all the spiritual stations and mystical states, and gathered them all in the present moment."

TS (A), p. 483

16. In reply to the question, "What is Sufism?", Rowaim said, "To remain steadfast upon the expanse, shunning expansiveness, and to be patient under the scourges, until the Way is traversed."

TS (A), p. 220

17. Abu Sahl Ṣa'luki: "Sufism is to eschew all criticism."

TS (A), p. 499

18. Shebli: "Sufism is the negating of humanity and the glorifying of Divinity."

TS (A), p. 171

19. Shebli: "Sufism's beginning is purity *(ṣafâ)* and its end is fidelity *(wafâ')*."

TS (A), p. 171

20. Asked to explain Sufism, Ya'qub Mozâbeli commented, "It is a state in which all human knowledge is negated."

TS (A), p. 275

21. Anṣâri: "Sufism can be realised neither by quietude nor by pursuit. It is the very Wrath of God, which like a lightning bolt of the Light of Divine Sublimity, descends from the All-High, striking whomever it will. It evades those who pursue it, while those to whom it is akin are pursued by it, however much they seek to escape it."

TS (A)

22. Sa'di: "What is the reality of Sufism?", one of the Shaikhs of Syria was asked. He replied, "Formerly, they were a company in the world who were dispersed outwardly, but were inwardly collected. At present, they are a group who appear collected outwardly, but who are inwardly dispersed."

G, II: 25

23. Bâbâ Ṭâher: "Sufism is immortal life, and a death devoid of life."[1]

KQ, p. 698

1. In translating this aphorism from Arabic into Persian, the author writes: "Sufism is life with God which is deathless, and death from vanity with no life nor backsliding into illusion."

24. Bâbâ Ṭâher: "Nothing can encompass Sufism, yet it encompasses everything. All things are for the sake of the Sufi, but he is for the sake of nothing."

TKQ, p. 703

25. Abu Ḥafṣ Ḥaddâd, when asked, "Who is a Sufi?" retorted, "The Sufi does not ask who a Sufi is."

NO, p. 178

26. Abu Bakr Kattâni: "The Sufi is a slave in appearance, but inwardly liberated and free."

NO, p. 177

27. Morta'esh: "Once I enquired about Sufism from Abu 'Abdo'llâh Ḥaḍhrami, who had observed for twenty years an absolute rule of silence. He answered me by citing the *Qoran:* 'Men who are true to what they have pledged in covenant with God.' (XXXIII: 23) 'What do the Sufis speak of?' I asked. He answered, 'Their eyes gaze wildly in astonishment and their hearts are bereft in terror.' (XIV: 43) 'What mystical state do they dwell in?' I enquired. He said, 'Firmly established in the favor of a Mighty King.' (LIV: 55) 'Say more,' I begged. He replied, 'Truly, the hearing and the sight and the heart — each of these will be held responsible.' (XVII: 36)."

NO, p. 120

28. A Master said: "All people profess faith in the One, yet cast themselves about on a thousand other thresholds. This sect declares 'One', and

abjures any other sign of themselves."

NO, p. 53

29. "A dog taught me Sufism," Shebli recounted. "When he was dozing in the courtyard of a house, the owner came out and drove him away. Unperturbed the dog returned. 'What a wretched cur,' I thought. As though by God's will, the brute became endowed with speech. 'Tell me, O Shaikh', he said, 'where else can I go, when he is my master?'"

TfA, I, p. 68

30. Ruzbehân: "Sufism is the consecration of one's innermost consciousness from all created things."

SS, p. 635

31. When Sahl 'Abdo'llâh was asked, "When does a man become a Sufi?" He replied, "Whenever his blood can be shed without impunity and his property confiscated lawfully, and when he views everything as coming from God, and perceives God's Mercy encompassing all creation." Ruzbehân comments: "The interpretation of these sayings is that the Sufi, on realizing Gnosis, views everything in a state of surrender to God's will. He doesn't allow himself to become entangled in sensing vexation towards God's creatures, either here or in the hereafter. He has freely forfeited, even with gratitude, his goods and his blood to God's creatures."

SS, p. 211

32. As the hour of Ḥallâj's rendezvous with death approached, Fâṭema Naishâburi asked the saint, "What is Sufism?"

"At the outset" declared Ḥallâj, "it is what you are observing, but what follows is concealed even to the adepts."

"This means," comments Ruzbehan, "that, at first, Sufism is attributed to 'me' but in the end it is only attributed to God who transcends all cognisance. In the beginning then, it is the annihilation of self, while ultimately it is subsistence in God."

SS, p. 390

33. When asked what Sufism is, Ḥallâj replied, "After attaining self-effacement, you arrive at the point where both effacement and affirmation cease to exist."

SS, p. 415

34. 'The science of Sufism is boundless and infinite, for it is bestowed by Divine Grace, rather than any amount of human effort. It is learned by inspiration, not through memorisation. Hence its grace is eternal, as it derives from a Being of infinite origin."

KST, p. 257

35. Anṣâri: "Teachers' of the Way, and Masters of Wisdom have declared that the work of Sufism is based upon emulation of the practices of the Companions of the Cave,[1] which were the

1. See *Qorân*, XVIII (The Cave)

following: one, self-examination and analysis of intention in actions; two, refinement of the will and aspiration; three, retirement from people; four, detachment from the pursuit of superfluities; five, sincerely inviting people to God and sincerity in repentence; six, liberation from the world's bondage; and seven, upon escape from subjugation to the ego, raising the hands of need in entreaty towards the precincts of the Self-Sufficient — burning, melting at times under the fury of God's Majesty, and at times glorying and delighting in the gentle breeze of Divine Intimacy."

TfA, II, p.10

36. Sohrawârdi Maqṭul: "The Sufi surmounts heaven and earth and is pre-eminent in all realms of Being."

MAS, p. 297

37. The biographer of Abu Sa'id Abe'l-Khair recounts: "Two travelers once visited the Master (Abu Sa'id) and asked to be instructed in Sufism. The Master rested his back against a pillar, placed his hand three times upon it, but said nothing. The pair paid their respects and took their leave. The wiser of the two asked his friend, 'Did you understand the Master's gesture?' 'No' said the other. 'The Master merely did what was required,' he explained; 'by laying hands upon the pillar, in three gestures, he instructed us to be silent, upright, and to shoulder our burdens'."

HS, p. 136

38. Abo'l-Ḥasan Nuri: "The Sufis are the

wisest of all people. All people were easily reconciled to His gratuities and graces, but the Sufis desired Him and His company alone, and settled for no surrogate. They were not selfishly impelled in their search for Him, rather they beheld a Vision, and riveted their eyes upon it. They could countenance nothing in exchange for God and abandoned all that was other than God. When all humanity was content with His Attributes, instead of the Attributor, they sought His Essence only. The whole world denied them, and those who were the more learned were the more fervent in voicing their denial."

TS (A), p. 62

39. Jonaid: "Sufism is sitting an hour without cares and worry with God." When asked what being without cares and worry meant, he replied, "It is discovery without search, and sight in which the seer cannot be distinguished from the seen."

TS (A), p. 168

40. Abo'l-Ḥasan Sirwâni: "Sufism is single-hearted concentration and solitude with God."

TS, p. 171

حال

IV

Mystical States

Mystical States

The literal meaning of the Arabic word *ḥâl* (pl:*aḥwâl)* is 'quality', 'condition', or 'shape'. As a technical term in Sufism, it refers to an influx of inspiration *(wâred)* which descends upon the heart of an aspirant without volition or effort on his part, as a result of devotion, invocation, or prayers of the heart. Resultant mystical states *(aḥwâl)* include joy and grief, contraction and expansion[1], and yearning and disquiet. As the name 'state' *(ḥâl)* itself implies, a 'mystical state' is impermanent, changeful in nature; its duration may last an hour, day or year.

States of a brief and evanescent nature have been labeled in various ways. Such terms as: 'flashes' *(lawâ'eḥ;* sing.: *lâ'eḥa)*, 'effulgence' *(lawâme',* sing.: *lâme'),* and auroral illuminations *(ṭawâle';* sing.: *ṭâle')* abound in the Sufi lexicon, being the visible outcome of nearness to the heart. Though the sun of gnosis *(ma'refat)* has not yet manifested itself to them, God grants their hearts spiritual sustenance through these fleeting states. While the firmament of neophytes' hearts, figuratively speaking, is still overcast by clouds of self-interest and sensuality, God may allow such states to glimmer like lanterns on the pathway before

1. For further detail concerning these two states see the author's *Sufism: Fear and Hope, Contraction and Expansion, Gathering and Dispersion, Intoxication and Sobriety, Annihilation and Subsistence.* (New York, 1982), Chap. II.

 them, rekindling their longing.

The following lights appear to novices:

1. 'Flashes' *(lawâ'eḥ)* resemble bolts of lightning which twinkle forth and then disperse.

2. 'Effulgence' *(lawâme')* is more pronounced in appearance than flashes, yet is not so swift to dissipate, lasting two to three moments. It tends to absorb one in God, and distance one from oneself.

3. 'Auroral illumination' *(ṭawâle')* is of a still and more pronounced appearance than effulgence and of longer duration.

The qualitative effect of these three genres of illumination depend upon an individual's receptivity. Sometimes their effect wears off immediately upon eclipse. Sometimes it lingers on — an ineffaceable experience full of grace, the revisitation of which becomes anticipated.

4. 'Striking lights', or 'nocturnal scintillations' *(ṭawâreq)* are of quite a weak radiance, resembling a glint of light infused *(wâred)* in the heart during supplicatory prayers at night, which may leave either an exhilarating or agonizing effect on the heart.

Two other mystical states, brief in span, are Divine 'infusions' *(wâredât)* in the heart, particular to both beginners and seekers midway on the Path. These are 'visitation' *(bawâda;* sing.: *bâ'ed)* and 'attack' *(hojum).* A visitation is a state which descends upon the heart from the supersensory realm *(ghaib)* proceeding from fear (of God) and arousing gladness or grief. An attack is a state which descends without the seeker's volition in the impact of the metaphysical moment[1] *(waqt)* upon the heart. Some seekers' states are visibly affected by a 'visitation' and 'attacks' easily overwhelm

1. See Chapter VI

them. Others are left apparently unmoved; they are appropriately refered to as 'masters of the moment', *(sâdât-e waqt).*

In reality, it would be more precise to designate flashes, effulgence, auroral illuminations, nocturnal scintillations, visitations and attack as *premonitions of states,* rather than actual mystical states. Sufi masters who have discussed this subject have often qualified these transitory premonitions as true mystical states. For example, Qoshairi cites Abo'l Ḥasan Ṣâyegh's definition in this respect: "Mystical states resemble lightning bolts. If they were to last, they would not be states, but only the provocations of the sensible faculties and the agitation of human nature."[1]

The above definition is eminently correct in my view, for were these premonitions to persist, their relevance would be distorted by the senses and imagination, reflexively having a hallucinatory and neurotic nature. Masters of the Path have just as often spoken of temporally continuous mystical states without reference to premonitions, an instance of which is Qoshairi's citation of this statement concerning mystical states by Abu 'Othmân':

"Forty years have passed in which God has not allowed me to fall into any state which could preoccupy me."[2]

This statement alludes to the unbroken continuity of the mystical state of contentment *(reḍhâ).*

1. RQ, pp. 68-69
2. Ibid., p. 93

Words of the Masters on Premonitions of Mystical States

I. Flashes *(lawâ'eḥ)*

Abdo'r-Razzâq Kâshâni: "*Lawâ'eḥ* is the plural of *lâ'eḥa* and is considered to denote a thing which is divulged to the senses from the imaginal world *('âlam-e methâl).*[1] This type of unveilment *(kash)* is formal *(ṣuri)* in appearance but in reality is a spiritual revelation from the All-Holy."

EO, p. 73

Ruzbehân: "*Lawâ'eḥ* are spiritual mysteries which radiate *(lâ'eḥa shawed)* transporting one to supernal degrees."

SS, p. 558

Hojwiri: *(Lawâ'eḥ* refers to the) "Affirmation of the object of desire, notwithstanding the advent of the negation thereof."

KM (trans), p. 385

Abdo'l-Razzâq Kâshâni: "*Lawâ'eḥ* is the exteriorisation of the incandescence of Divine revelation. If it swiftly dwindles away, it is called merely a ray of lightning *(bâreqa)* or transitory intuition *(khâṭera).*"

RSh, IV, p. 48

1. The world of subtle autonomous spiritual forms where "what is corporeal becomes spirit and what is spiritual assumes a body" in Najmo'd-Din Kobrâ's words, cited by H. Corbin in *The Man of Light in Iranian Sufism*, (trans. N. Pearson, London, 1982), p.106.

Shah Ne'mato'llâh: "According to one school, *lawâ'eḥ* is the manifestation of the lights of the mysteries of inner consciousness *(bâṭen)*, as well as mystical progression from state to state. In our opinion, it is a light which radiates from the lights of the Essence and the Divine Visage, in order to affirm rather than negate, illuminating the non-corporeal eye.

"With the apparition of flashes in a contemplative state, a trace of the Divine Names is beheld; a mystical progression from a lower to a higher state is witnessed. If there be no progression, the term 'flash' is not applied to the Lights of the Divine Attributes, even if the mystical state be genuine. Mystical states are Divine gifts and a kind of influx *(wâredat)*, whereas spiritual stations are acquired by the application of effort. One of the prerequisites of flashes is that they be comprehended by the (non-corporeal) eye, pertaining to the psyche *(nafs)* rather than by inner vision *(baṣirat)*.

"It is said that someone asked the Prophet, 'Do you see your Lord?' He answered, 'It is a radiance I see.' The interpretation being that the bodily eye cannot view that Divine Light, but only a light formed in a special manner. "Vision comprehends Him not, but He comprehends all vision." (VI:103)

"Only if the Absolute Light becomes visible throughout all the hierarchical levels of Being is vision of Him conceivable, and only when on the Western horizons of these levels, the sun of God's hidden Ipseity *(howiyat)* sets, will the sources of the [spiritual] stars on the Divine Names and Attributes be imbued with grace. The Absolute Light cannot be visibly apprehended by any organ of cognition, for "naught is as His likeness, and He is the Hearer, the Seer." (XLII:11)

"Though Life, Knowledge, Power, Volition,

 Audition, Vision, and Speech are Attributes of God — Attributes with which creatures may be qualified — nonetheless, these Attributes have different relations to creature and Creator. In fact, the relationship of God and Man to these Attributes is utterly contrary. One who perceives flashes comprehends this vision intelligently (i.e. sees and *knows)*. One who only sees without knowing lacks realisation. Seeing is common, but knowing is reserved for the elect."

RSh, IV p. 222

Shah Ne'mato'llâh: "To men of God, 'flashes' denote the theophany of the lights of the Divine Essence and His Countenance of Glory to an eye unbridled by physicality, in affirmation rather than negation. Each Divine Name has a certain effect; these Divine Names radiate during contemplation of their effects."

RSh, II p. 385

Ruzbehân: " 'Flashes' excell effulgence *(lawâme')* in perfection. Whereas effulgence is the source of all revelation, flashes indicate the triumph of the Sultan of the illumination of the radiant moons of the Divine Attributes. The verity of the spiritual pull manifested by flashes causes their brilliance to illumine the hearts of mystics purified of the opaquity of created being, so as to enhance the intimacy of their spiritual degree, proximity, and contemplative vision. Yet flashes are unsteady, concealing themselves in the state of contraction and revealing themselves in the state of expansion. Their character is such that the lover may reach the station of Love's perfection, become absorbed in the depths of Divine Nearness, and witness His tremendous Majesty *(jalâl)* through His fascinating Beauty *(jamâl)*. He beholds the hidden mysteries of the angelic realm and the Divine Acts and apprehends the invisible arcanum hidden to all hearts.

"As a gnostic said: 'flashes are lights of unveilment *(tajalli)* by means of which the truths of the sacred sciences illuminate all intelligences'."

MA, p. 98

II. Effulgence *(lawâme')*

Tahanawi: "As a technical term in Sufism 'effulgence' refers to radiant lights which shine upon novices pure in soul. Their light is reflected from the imagination *(khiyâl)* to the *sensus communis (ḥess-e moshtarek)*[1] and finally apprehended by the external senses.

KF, II, p. 1299

Abdo'r-Razzâq Kâshâni, after citing the above definition, adds: "Lights resembling the sun, moon, and stars are subsequently seen, seeming to illuminate their surroundings. If these brilliant lights come by way of the prevalence of the Lights of Divine Grace and Bounty, they are green in colour."

ES, p. 74

1. According to Avicenna's psychology, this is the faculty which collects and analyses the data conveyed by the sense-organs to the ordinary consciousness. His system was later adopted by the medieval Jewish and Latin Christian scholastic theologians, from which we get the modern English 'common sense'.

Ruzbehân: *"Lawâme'* are supersensory lights which reveal themselves to the heart, by which the pathways of wisdom are recognised."

SS, p. 558

Hojwiri: "Effulgence denotes the manifestation of spiritual light to the heart, with the sustained subsistence of its benefits."

KM (orig.) p. 500

Ruzbehân: *"Lawâme'* are rays of light which radiate in the initial stages of contemplation. Each effulgance shines — for a brief moment of rapture, preceeded by a bolt of lightning *(barq)* and tempered by a certain spiritual trait *(kholq)*. Each trait, in progression on the Way, is imbued with a particular observed form *(rasm)*, acting as a mirror of the lover's face, where the distinctive features of his mystical state are displayed. One gnostic described effulgence as the 'shimmering illumination of the Divine Attributes which appear in the wellspring of the Divine Essence through deeds carried out in the abodes of Love'."

MA, p. 98

III. Auroral Illumination. *(ṭawâle')*

Abdo'r-Razzâq Kâshâni: "Auroral illumination occurs in the form of lights which appear at the outset of the theophany of Divine Names, in the inward consciousness *(bâṭen)* of the devotee, the illumination of which embellishes his personality and character."

ES, p. 64

Ruzbehân: "Auroral illumination represents the lights of Divine Oneness, which enter the gnostic's heart, their radiance extinguishing all the lights of intelligence and cognition. The source of auroral illumination *('asl-e ṭawâle')* is the rising of the suns of revelation and the moons of the Attributes in the heart of unitarians *(mowaḥḥedân),* whose awesome majesty wrings all illumination from the stars ablaze with faith and gnosis."

SS, p. 556

Hojwiri: "By *ṭawâle'* is signified the appearence of the splendours of mystical knowledge in the heart."

KM (trans.), p. 385

IV. Visitations *(bawâdah)*

'Abdo'r-Razzâq Kâshâni: "Visitations are a phenomenon which suddenly comes over the heart from the Invisible *(ghaib)* and cause its expansion or contraction."

ES, p. 38

V. Attack *(hojum)*

Ruzbehân: " 'Attack' indicates a deluge of mystical states, the animation of one's esoteric consciousness *(asrâr)*, the inrush of spirits towards the angelic pleroma *(malakut)* and their undaunted

74 convergence upon the Divine Lights."

SS, p. 553

Premonitions of Mystical States According to Qoshairi

'Flashes', 'effulgence' and 'auroral illumination' are all terms which are similar in meaning, and almost identical, insofar as they are all preliminary states characteristic of beginners, who experience them through proximity to the heart. God nurtures their hearts as the moment *(waqt)* requires, through these premonitions, "wherein they have food for the morning and the evening,[1] though the sun of mystical cognition has not yet granted them total enlightenment. Whenever the sky of their hearts becomes overclouded by the mist of sensual pleasures, a ray of revelation *(kashf)*, flashes, or effulgence of Divine Nearness emanates, and in their darkened, veiled state they await the sight of flashes.

At first flashes appear, then, successively, effulgence and auroral illumination. Flashes are rays of light which appear and fade away. Effulgence is more evident, clearer than flashes, and slower to dissipate, lasting two to three 'moments'. The appearance of effulgence severs 'you' from 'you', and unites you to itself, or

1. Qoran: XIX: 62. The entire verse alludes exoterically to the denizens of Eden, but esoterically to the heaven of the heart.

figuratively expressed: 'the daylight persists, but the armies of night mount an attack.'

Auroral illumination has a more sustained appearance, its rays cut through the penumbra more sharply, while its sway is more marked than the preceeding premonitions. Yet, being of variable duration, it may dwindle at any moment. One always dreads its departure, even though its abatement is protracted. The aforesaid descriptions vary according to context of course.

Of some of these premonitions no effect is left, as only what appears to be the perpetual darkness of the night sky remains when the planets set. Others leave a trace of themselves; although their exterior appearance vanishes, a nostalgic pain is left in their stead, and though their light dissipates, a glow lingers on. After their awesome Divine ascendancy *(ghâlebat)* abates, the aspirant lives on through the grace of their radiance. Consoled during moments of contemplation, he exists in anticipation of the recurrence of these prefatory rays of vision.

'Visitations' and 'attacks' belong to mystical states of this category as well. Visitations constitute a state which suddenly descends upon the heart from the supersensory realm, arousing gladness or grief. 'Attack' is an involuntary state which descends by force of the 'metaphysical moment' *(waqt)* upon the heart, its appearance pronounced as befits the strength or weakness of the individual. Some seekers' states are visibly affected by 'visitations' while attacks overcome them as well. Others are left apparently unmoved, and hence are appropriately named 'masters of the moment' *(sâdât-e waqt)*."

RQ, p. 119

When, like a bud's in-broken, crumpled petal
Our hearts are contracted, inwardly withdrawn,
What story is left for the courier zephyr's
Windy narration to convey?

Ḥâfeẓ

1. 'Abdo'r-Razzâq Kâshani: "Mystical states are Divine Gifts which descend upon the heart, and are not occasioned by one's own efforts and endeavours. They include grief *(ḥosn)*, fear *(khauf)*, contraction *(qabḍh)* expansion *(basṭ)*, yearning *(shauq)*, and mystic intuition *(dhauq)*. Insofar as the soul's base qualities come to light, *ḥâl*[1] disperses, whether a state of like nature should happen to follow it or not. If a state should endure or come to 'belong' to the Sufi, it is termed a 'station' *(maqâm)*."

EO, p. 57

2. Abu 'Omar Zojâji: "Whenever someone speaks of a state without realisation, his words do a disservice to the listener, for his statements are only pretentions which sweep away his heart's vision, in which case God prohibits his realisation of that state."

RQ, p. 78

1. *Ḥâl* [(a collective nouṇ in Persian and Arabic, but an enumerative noun in English] is the singular of *'aḥwâl* (mystical states). It is a generic term used to refer to either a mystical state as an abstract condition, a particular mystical state, or the quantity of spiritual feeling within a mystic's soul — i.e. mystical consciounsess (the meaning here).

3. Abu 'Omar ebn Nojaid: "Any state which is not the outcome of knowledge *('elm)* is more detrimental than beneficial to its possessor."

RQ, p. 79

4. Ruzbehân: "*Ḥâl* is a Divine inspiration from the Invisible, granted to people of the heart *(ahl-e del)* which transforms them beyond the qualities of humanity."

MA, p. 86

5. Ruzbehân: "The phenomenon of *ḥâl* involves the suden visualisation of a Divine quality in the heart, beyond all recognisable trappings of tradition."

MA, p. 86

6. Commenting on the saying of Mohammad: 'I swear by God that each day seventy times I seek God's forgiveness and turn back towards Him',[1] Abu 'Ali Daqqâq explained, "The Prophet was invariably in a state of mystical progress *(taraqqi)*. In advancing from a lower to a higher state, he looked back at times upon his former states which he reckoned in retrospect, as turbid and without lustre. Because the providential quantity of God's grace is unlimited, such states, likewise, are endless."

RQ, p 94

7. Ghazâli: "Some of the Masters of Khorasan have said: 'Mystical states are the products of

1. *Jâme' Ṣaghir,* Vol. I, p. 103

 meritorious deeds *('amal)'.*"

EO, Vol.5, p. 225

8. 'Ezzo'd-Din Mahmud Kâshâni: *"Ḥâl* is an infusion of inspiration *(wâred)* which from time to time descends upon the heart from the Supernal World. Such occurrences are intermittent until such time as one becomes enraptured by Divine Attraction and elevated from a humble to an exalted station."

MH; p. 125

9. Jonaid: *"Ḥâl* is an infusion of inspiration in the heart which is impermanent."[1]

MH, p. 125

10. Hojwiri: "Ḥâreth Moḥâsebi maintained that a 'state' may be permanent, and argued that love and longing and contraction and expansion are states; if they cannot be permanent, then the lover would not be a lover, and until man's state becomes his attribute *(ṣefat)* that state cannot properly be ascribed to him."

KM, (trans.) p. 181

11. Hojwiri: "The tongue of the possessor of *ḥâl* is silent concerning his *ḥâl,* but his actions proclaim the reality of that *ḥâl.* In the light of this, a certain spiritual director said, 'To ask about *ḥâl* is absurd, because *ḥâl* is the annihilation of speech *(maqâl).*"

KM (trans.), p. 369-70

1. Jonaid is alluding to premonitions of states in this statement, rather than the states themselves. (Author's note)

12. Hojwiri: "Masters who maintained the impermanence of mystical states have reasoned that 'states are like their names', i.e. they vanish almost as soon as they descend and unite themselves with the heart. Whatever is permanent becomes an attribute, and attributes subsist in an object which must be more perfect than the attributes themselves; and this reduces the doctrine that 'states' are permanent to an absurdity."

KM, (trans.) p. 182

13. Ruzbehân: "*Ḥâl* denotes the infusion of supersensory lights in the heart, rendering one's contemplative moments *(waqt)* free of impurity. *Ḥâl* as such, is an unmeditated theophany, the revelation of God by way of the mystery of the Spirit, without the exercise of personal effort or formal discipline."

SS, p. 546

14. Abdo'r-Razzâq Kâshâni: "Mystical states are a Divine gift showered upon the servant by the Lord. Gifts are given as a reward for meritorious deeds, for purity of heart and for mortification of the passions.

"Mystical states *('aḥwâl),* literally 'alternation' or 'transmutation', are so named because they indicate the transmutation *(taḥwil)* of all that is conferred *(moḥawwel,* literally 'changed over') upon the servant — that is to say, the traits of humanity in its alienation from the Divine — back into Divine qualities, bringing propinquity to the Divine. This is the real meaning of evolution *(taraqqi).*"

RSh, IV, p. 8

15. Jorjâni: *"Ḥâl* literally signifies the culmination of the past, and the inception of the future. To mystics *('ahl-e ḥaqq)* the term designates spiritual meanings *(ma'âni)* which cross the heart without volitional acquisition, artifice, or self-consciousness. Joy *(ṭarab)*, grief *(ḥozn)*, contraction *(qabḍh)* and expansion are thus typified as *ḥâl.*

"Insofar as the soul's bad qualities come to light, *ḥâl* disperses, whether or not a state of like nature should follow it. If the state endures and comes to 'belong' to the Sufi, it is termed a 'station' *(maqâm)*. While stations are acquired by diligent effort and spiritual combat *(mojâhadat)*, states are Divine gifts, arising from the wellspring of Divine generosity."

TJ, p. 55

مقام

V

Spiritual Stations

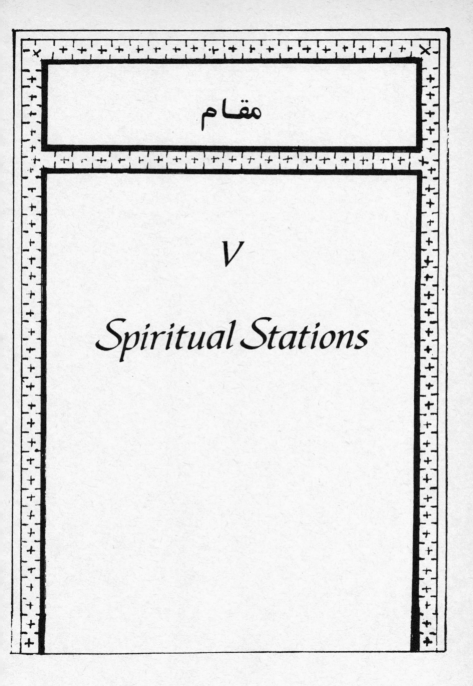

Spiritual Stations

With all my boasting about prescience,
  miracle-working and stations,
I was never vouchsafed
  realisation of any station.

Ḥâfeẓ

The Arabic world *moqâm* is a gerund meaning 'standing', while *maqâm* denotes the place where the standing takes place, i.e., 'station'. As a technical term in Sufism, realisation of a particular station comes through proper observance of the rules pertaining thereunto, and a sort of conquest of its trials, and the exercise of a certain ascetic endeavour. It is said that no station can be effectively realised except through Divine confirmation, if one's efforts are to have a proper foundation.

Spiritual Stations According to the Masters

1. Abdo'r-Razzâq Kâshâni: "A station is realised when the devotee becomes characterised by the perfections of the Divine Name it exemplifies; correspondingly, failure to achieve the perfection of the station possessed by the aspirant hinders his progress to a higher station. Just as it is

 unsuitable for one who has not yet realised the perfections of acquiescence to the Divine Will *(qanâ'at)* to be qualified with the perfections of trust in God *(tawwakol),* likewise it is wrong to ascribe submission *(taslim)* to one who has not yet attained the virtues of trust in God. Further examples of this nature abound.

"Realisation of a station *(estifâ')* does not involve the aspirant being deprived of the effects of a lower station in the process of ascending to a higher one; on the contrary, the overall effects and the eminent degrees of the lesser station are comprised in the higher station as well. For a station to be realised, the aspirant must 'possess' it, that is to say, be firmly grounded in it, in such a fashion that it becomes his very mystical consciousness *(ḥâl).* Only true realisation of its meaning entitles the aspirant to its name. Thus when he is termed 'acquiescent' or 'reliant', then reality truly corresponds with the name. The aspirant merits a station only through his spiritual 'standing' *('eqâmat)* there."

ES, p. 87

2. Abu Naṣr Sarrâj: "The term 'station' designates a devotee's 'standing' before God in accordance to his arising for acts of devotion, spiritual combat, ascetic discipline and self-denial. God announces, 'This is for whoever fears My Station and My Threatening.' (XIV:14)"

LT, p. 41

3. Bâbâ Ṭâher: "Stations are for weaklings who have contented themselves with the station attained, because they are spiritually impotent to

traverse the stations beyond, whereas the elect are 'in the favour of a Mighty King.' (LIV: 55)"

TKQ, p. 563

4. 'Ezzo'd-din Mahmud Kâshâni: "The concept of *maqâm* designates one of the numerous gradations of spiritual progress which represents the ground covered in the seeker's advance and wherein he abides. While mystical states pertain to what is above the seeker, not subject to his control — his whole being subject to their sway, spiritual stations are the loci of his subjugation. Just as there is no station which is wholly uninfiltrated by a state, neither is there a state which is far removed from some station."

MH, p. 125

5. Ruzbehân: "The devotee's object of anticipation is a spiritual station such as patience *(ṣabr)* or gratitude *(shokr)*. Attaining its perfections, he is recognised as the 'holder' of a station *(ṣâḥeb maqâm)*. Yet beyond this station lies a further station, for 'there is not one of us but has his known station' (XXXVII:164). Realisation of a spiritual station in essence involves qualification with Divine qualities in the very midst of the fluctuation *(talwin)* of mystical states."

SS, p. 547

Ḥâl and Maqâm: Some Definitions and Distinctions by the Masters

1. Hojwiri: "The term 'station' denotes the way of

 the seeker, his progress in the field of endeavour, and his rank before God in accordance with his merit; the term 'state' denotes the favour and grace which God bestows upon the heart of His servant, unconnected with any spiritual combat which the devotee may have practised.

'Station' belongs to the category of acts, 'state' to the category of gifts. Hence the man that has a 'station' stands by his own spiritual struggle, whereas the man that has a 'state' is dead to 'self' and stands by a 'state' which God creates in him."

KM (trans.), p. 181

2. Najmo'd-Din Kobrâ: "Mystical states serve as alimentation and sustenance for the aspirant's spiritual journey, and are the steed upon which he mounts to be carried towards the object of his search, for travel without provisions is unlawful. Stations, as rest areas and places of descent, serve to ease the stress of travel. Mystical states are accessories of the Way; spiritual stations are the rest-houses provided for the travelers thereon. It might be said that *ḥâl* provides wings for the bird and *maqâm*, the nest."

FJ

3. "Mystical states are Divine gifts, while stations are dependent on effort. States stem from the quintessence of Divine munificence; stations are Divine favours earned through work. The possessor of a state progresses higher, whereas the possessor of a station abides therein."

RQ, p. 92

4. Hojwiri, in describing the doctrine of Moḥâsebi, writes: "You must know that satisfaction is the end of 'stations' and the beginning of 'states'; it is a place of which one side rests on acquisition and effort, and the other side on love and rapture; there is no 'station' above it. At this point spiritual struggle *(mojâhedât)* ceases. Hence its beginning is in the class of things Divinely bestowed. It is presumed that one who, in the beginning, saw his satisfaction through himself declared it a station, whereas one who, in the end, saw his satisfaction through God, declared it to be a state."

KM (trans., slightly modified), p. 182

5. 'Ezzo'd-Din Mahmud Kâshâni: "What one master regarded as a state, another viewed as a station, insofar as all stations are initially states, then become stations, hence from this arose their divergence of opinion in the matter. It may be observed, for instance, how repentance *(tauba)*, self-examination *(moḥâsebe)*, and contemplation *(morâqebe)* are only states at first, subject to fluctuation and passing, but when approached by efforts at acquisition become stations. States are encompassed by what can be acquired by effort, whereas stations are surrounded by Divine gifts. This distinction however exists: that in mystical states, Divine favour is obvious and human effort is hidden, while in spiritual stations, human effort is obvious and Divine favour hidden.

"A further controversy of the Sufis concerns whether or not it is possible for the aspirant to perfect the station wherein he abides before proceeding to the next station.

"Jonaid was of the opinion that it is possible for a devotee to rise to a higher state before achieving perfection of a lower state, though remnants of the antecedent state still bind him. From the standpoint of the higher state he may comprehend the state below and perfect it.[1]

"According to Anṣâri, a given station may be perfected only through accession to a higher station, from which standpoint the aspirant may comprehend and, thus, complete the lower.

"Shehâbo'd-Din Sohrawardi believed it impossible for an aspirant to advance to a higher station before perfecting the station where he is. Before his upward progress, however, he is granted a mystical state from the higher station, by the grace of which he is afforded a direct advance. In this way his movement forward is accomplished from station to station by Divine Will, rather than through his own efforts. This mutual accommodation of God to the devotee and the devotee to God may be inferred from the sacred tradition: 'If my devotee approaches Me by as much as one hand's length, I approach him by a cubit,[2] whereby this doctrine may be seen to be in accordance with orthodox tradition. The aspirant's progress through exercise of his own will evokes the attractive force of the Divine Will in the guise of mystical states."

MH, p. 128

6. Rumi writes:

Like the initial display of a beautiful bride
mystical states shadow forth, where stations

1. This remark is true also of stations. (Author's note)
2. Recorded in the *Mosnad* of Ahmad ebn Ḥanbal, (Egypt: 1313 A.H.) Vol.II, p.251

in mystical solitude abide.
The formal pageantry of mystical feelings
is beheld by commoners and Kings alike,
and seen by all and sundry;
Kings alone are endeared to
that unveiled spectacle of Her,
the rite of conjugal seclusion.
Though countless sufis and adepts abound
acquainted with mystical states,
rare is the mystic akin to any station.

MM, I: 1435-8

'Position' and 'Stopping-point'

The concept of 'position' *(waqfa)* is another technical term of the Sufis. According to 'Abdo'r-Razzaq Kashani: "The term 'position' signifies a halting place between two stations, where the aspirant pauses to amend the remnants of the prior station and prepares to ascend to the station beyond."

ES, p. 54

A further category is 'stopping-point' *(mauqef)*. Shah Ne'mato'llâh writes: "In the theosopher's terminology, the 'stopping-point' designates the penultimate station, augurring the glory of the forthcoming and ultimate station. Amongst ecstatics, it alludes to the station of perfection in two respects: firstly, with respect to the two other stations on either side of it, where it is characterised as the 'Comprehensive Isthmus' *(barzakhe jâme')*, and secondly, with respect to itself exclusively, where it is termed the 'Supreme Isthmus' *(barzakh al-barâzekh).* The Comprehensive Isthmus embraces both Necessary and Possible Being."

RSh, II, p. 303

وقت

VI

Metaphysical Time

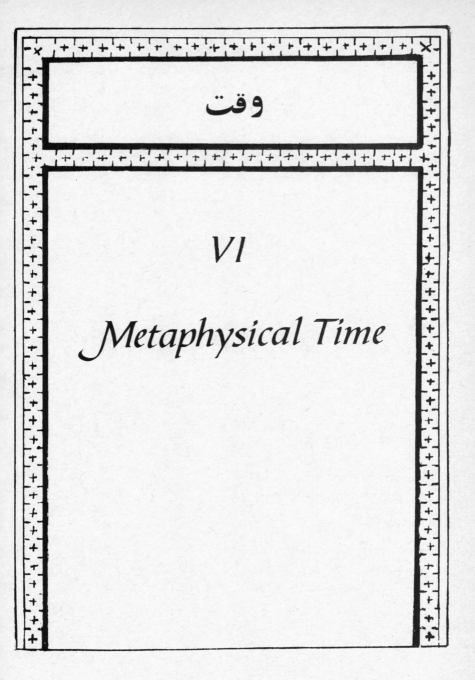

Waqt: Metaphysical Time[1]

Red roses have blossomed,
Nightingales are all drunk
Everywhere, the hue-and-cry of ecstasy
O Sufi
devotee
of the Eternal Now!

Ḥâfeẓ

The literal meaning of *waqt* is: time, hour, occasion or instance. The Prophet of Islam pronounced: "I have a time with God that no archangel or previous prophet can share."[2]

Waqt as a technical term in Sufism is a word used to characterise an influx of inspiration, or the evocation of rapture at the present moment from the Divine within the heart, which 'plucks' the Sufi outside the serial process of past and future time.

Striving to be engaged with God at every instant, the Sufi regards the present moment as

1. Perhaps better translated as 'a moment of eternity' or the 'Eternal Now' *(nunc aeternum)*. R.A. Nicholson in the majority of his texts translated from Arabic and Persian renders *waqt* as simply *time*. According to the context we have translated this term as 'time' or 'moment', and sometimes simply transcribed the term *waqt*. Therefore the reader should be aware that all references hereafter in this translation to 'time', 'moment' or 'eternal now', *without* the qualifying 'metaphysical' *all consistently* indicate the term *waqt* in the original.
2. See the Author's *Traditions of the Prophet (Aḥadith)* Vol I. (N.Y. 1981) p.31

particularly precious. His consciousness as a result, is not obsessed by the past or the future, and remembering the Divine, he rejoices in heart. Allowing himself to fancy the future or the past, the Sufi believes, will obscure his focus on the Truth, and camouflage his *waqt*. Thus Abu Sa'id Kharraz advised, "Do not occupy your precious time except with the most precious of things, and the most precious thing for a devotee is that deed in which he engages himself between the past and the future."[1] Needless to say, the Sufi's most precious possession is remembrance of Reality, of the Beloved.

According to Hojwiri, "The times *(auqât)* of the mystics of unitarian persuasion, are actually two, one accompanying a state of 'loss' *(faqd)* and one accompanying a state of 'gain' *(wajd)*, one in the place of union and one in the place of separation. At both these times he is overwhelmed, because both his union and his separation are brought about by God, without such volition or acquisition on the devotee's part, as would make it possible to characterise him in any way."

KM, (trans.), p. 368
(with minor changes).

Different Meanings of Waqt

Waqt has several distinct meanings as follows:

1. *Waqt* functions as a 'container' of time *(zamân)* for Divinely inspired mystical states which overwhelm the heart. In the technical language of the Sufis two kinds of such containers are distinguished: a) a stationary container which

1. The two foregoing paragraphs were freely adapted from Hojwiri. KM (orig.) p.480

is referred to as 'place', and b) a mobile container, which is referred to as 'time'.

Adapted from
TKQ, p. 644

2. If an imagined event is brought about by a real, actual event, the latter is said to be 'time' *(waqt)* in relation to the former.

For example, if one says "I shall visit you on the first of the month," your visit is purely imaginary; you may or may not visit. 'The first of the month', however, is a real event, because when this month passes, the first of the next month will come. Therefore, 'the first of next month' is a real event relative to one's arrival.

The Conditions of Time

Lest the moment *(waqt)* go to waste, it must be treated properly. In this respect, there are primarily three conditions which should be taken into account:

1. The Conservation of Time: *Waqt* must be protected by the Sufi from the ego's intrusive meddling. Furthermore, one should not engage in reflection upon *waqt* during *waqt*, if the purity of *waqt* is to be preserved.

2. The Law of Time: A Sufi should not allow himself to become constrained by *waqt*, nor fall prey to pride, nor indulge in self-display.

3. The Hiding of Time: Within the duration of his *waqt*, the mystical state of the Sufi should be

 discreetly concealed from others.

Adapted from TKQ,
pp. 645-46

Losing and Gaining Time

For a Sufi, time *(waqt)* which is spent in the absence of self, void of ego-consciouness, is considered 'gain' and 'profit' whereas time spent with the involvement of self, is considered 'waste' and 'loss'.

Adapted from TKQ,
p. 655

Distinctions between *Ḥâl and Waqt*

Hojwiri writes:

"No man can attain the reality of *waqt* by the application of effort, for *waqt* is something that does not come within the scope of human acquisition. The masters have said, 'Time is a cutting sword', because it is characteristic of a sword to cut, and *waqt* cuts the root of both future and past.

"*Ḥâl* is that which descends upon the moment *(waqt)*, which it adorns as the spirit adorns the body. *Waqt* has need of *ḥâl*, for *waqt* is beautified by *hâl* and subsists thereby. When the 'possessor' of *waqt* comes into the possession of *ḥâl*, he is no longer subject to change, being more steadfast in his spiritual development; for when he has *waqt* without *ḥâl*, he may lose it, but when *ḥâl* attaches itself to him, his whole spiritual life is transformed into *waqt* and that cannot be lost. Just as formerly *waqt* descended upon him while he abided in forgetfulness *(gheflat),* now he abides in *waqt* and is visited by *ḥâl.* For the possessor of *waqt* may become forgetful, but the possessor of *hâl* cannot possibly be so."

KM, (trans., slightly modified), p. 369

Hojwiri subsequently cites Abu 'Ali Daqqâq's subtle statement concerning the reality of *waqt:*

"In this world and the next, whether you are happy or unhappy, whenever and wherever you are, is *waqt. Ḥâl,* however, is different, for it is an inspiration which comes from God to the devotee, and banishes all of this from the heart."

KM,(trans.), p. 463

Lastly, Hojwiri notes:

"Ḥâl is thus a quality of masters, and *waqt* the degree of a disciple. The latter being fundamentally with himself, finds periodic delight in *waqt,* while the former, in the expanse of *ḥâl,* is principally with God."

KM,(orig.), p. 484

The Distinction between Time and Breath

Waqt as a technical term among the Sufis sometimes refers to the sudden unveiling of a mystical state from the Unseen, which seizes and strips the Sufi of his ordinary consciousness. Thus defined, *waqt* bears some relation to breath *(nafas),* another term used by the Sufi. This connection is described by 'Ezzod'd-Din Maḥmud Kâshâni as follows:

"'Breath' designates the overall permanence of a contemplative state, the perpetuation of which serves to succour the hearts of adepts in love, in the same way that the sustaining of the flesh depends upon the grace of continued respiration. Were the corporeal heart deprived for an hour of the vitalising effect of respiration, the intense heat of the body would cause the heart to catch fire. In the same way, if the essence of the yearning lover's heart were excluded for a flash or a moment from the vision of the Beloved, the flames of his ardent yearning would soon consume him.

"And the difference between 'breath' and 'time' is that time is a mystical state which is realised irregularly, at short intervals, as a rapture which alternatively discloses and conceals itself. Breath, on the other hand, is a state unpunctuated by pauses or intervals, whence the proverb, 'Time is for novices, while breath belongs to the adepts'."

MH, p. 141

Idioms Relating to Time in the Sufi Lexicon

1. 'Presence in the Moment' (*ḥâḍher-e waqt budan)*

The Sufi should strive to live in the present moment, to be vigilantly observant of *waqt*. Whatever happens to him at a given moment through God's Will, not by his own contrivance, should be greeted with acquiescence, but where it is clear that individual volition must be exercised, the wisest course should be chosen.

2. The 'Child of the Moment' *(ebn al-waqt)*

Sufis have long since recognised that attention and attachment to the past, and living in it, is literally, a 'waste of time', just as reflection upon the future is a forfeiture of the present. The Sufi, in fact, is a 'child of the moment'; clutching like a child to the hem of the mantle of his father: 'Time', he lives spontaneously, considering the present instant most precious. He busies himself in the most constructive way, lest his 'time go to waste.' Rumi's usage of this idiom is exemplified in two verses:

The Sufi is 'a son of the moment;'
The word *manana* is unheard of
on the Way

MM, I: 133

The Sufi is 'a son of the moment,'
In quest of purity; he holds the moment
close, like a son clings to his father.

MM, III: 1433

3. The 'Father of the Moment' *(abo'l-waqt)*
This term, according to some Sufis, designates an individual who is in control of 'time'. *Waqt* is subject to his will, which he occupies in the best and most beneficial of works.

4. Being 'at the Moment's Behest' *(be ḥokm-e waqt)*
This expression describes the state of the Sufi who, at a given moment, possesses no free will before the Divine Will, having surrendered and committed himself to the Beloved's behest.

5. 'In Subjection to Time' *(dar taṣarrof-e waqt)*

If within a *waqt*, the Sufi seeks from God to please himself, time will overwhelm him, and prevail over him and become his veil. He will be 'subjected to time'. If the Sufi, on the contrary, during such a moment pursues the Truth, the Truth he becomes the veil of time and subjects it to himself.

Adapted from TKQ, p. 646

6. 'Understanding Time' *(waqt-shenâsi)*

Sufis use this expression to express the value of each moment and warn against the wasting of time. In this regard, Ḥâfeẓ cautions the reader:

The heart misunderstands
the measure of time,
the moment's worth;
It stands by idle —
Alas! When we regret at last
All these unreaped minutes.

And elsewhere enjoins:

Rise and come!
The *waqt*-cognisant
Earth and heaven sell freely
For an idol's company and a cup
of drossless wine.

7. 'Understanding What Suits the Moment' *(maṣleḥat-e waqt)*

This phrase among the Sufis simply alludes to the pragmatic principle of following on every occasion the most expedient course of conduct. Ḥâfeẓ says, for example:

The moment is best served so far as I can see
if I shift off to the tavern
and seat myself there - carefree and cheerhearted.

Or:

O rose,
I wonder at your benevolence
In bearing the thorn's company;
Such gallantry I suppose you see
Suits the moment best.

8. 'Time's Currency' *(naqd-e waqt)*

In the works of Najmo'd-Din Razi, this expression carries a twofold significance:

i.) Eating and drinking in the present. Razi relates, "They abandon themselves like brutes and beasts to the currency of time, and are, thus, debarred from all feeling of mystic experience and all relish for the spiritual stations realised by men."

ME, p. 30

ii.) 'Rubbing Time's Coin Upon a Touchstone.'

"An explanation has been presented (in this book) of the perfections and privations of humankind along with the nurture and development of the human being in every condition relative to mystical states and spiritual stations. Perhaps those who have pretentions of embarking on this Way, as well as adepts in gnosis and spiritual progress, when rubbing the coin of their time upon the touchstone of this text, may find a sign of such stations within themselves, and so become elated and hopeful that they have actually stepped upon the way of God. If, on the other hand, they should perceive no trace of such a reality within themselves, they must not allow themselves to fall prey to egoistic pride or Satanic delusions. Rather they should cast out all proud notions from their minds and set forth on the high road of the mystic quest with piety and not become inflated by a few rotten words."

ME, p. 30

9. 'Under the Sway of the Moment' *(ghâlebat-e waqt)*

Because novices in Sufism are most often preoccupied with *waqt,* to the point of being enthralled by it, their state is characterised as being under the sway of the moment. This expression is used in this context for example, by Najmo'd-Din Razi (ME, p.325) in describing the spiritual experiences of Abu Sa'id Abe'l-Khair as a youth.[1]

10. The 'Brothers of the Moment'. *(akhawân-waqt)*

Certain Sufi masters specifically devoted themselves to the establishment of sessions of *samâ'* (audition to spiritual music and singing).[2] The value of these moments, being occasions of intense concentration on God, was stressed. Such masters and their disciples came to be known as 'brothers of the moment' since they endeavoured to make the maximum use of the ever present 'metaphysical moment', with its associated realisation of states of ecstasy and grace. Aflâki's description of *samâ'* in his biography of Jalâlo'd-Din Rumi, the *Manâqeb al-'ârefin,* shows an example of this usage:

1. For an account of his biography see: R.A. Nicholson's *Studies in Islamic Mysticism* (Cambridge, 1921)
2. The reader is referred to the author's: *In the Tavern of Ruin* (N.Y. 1978), Chap. IV, for a further description of *samâ'*.

"In the house of the governor, it is related, a grand *samâ'* was sponsored. The notables of the day, who were 'brothers of the moment', were assembled. Our master, Sadro'd-Din, went into a rapture and extemporaneously composed this quatrain:

Without you, who knows the infirm
from the strong vowels; who fathoms verses
said to be 'inspired'?

Who may resolve — O decoder of mysteries
without you, the subtleties
secreted in any research?

Deeply moved, he rubbed his face in the dust before Rumi's feet, moaning like a lover, acclaiming in glowing terms the soul-vivifying effect of the company present."

MA, p. 601

11. 'Masters of the Moment' *(sâdât-e waqt)*
"Sufis whose mystical states are not visibly altered by 'visitations' *(bawâda)* or an 'attack' *(hojum)* are named 'masters of the moment.' "

RQ, p. 119

Words of the Masters on *Waqt*

1. 'Abdo'r-Razzâq Kâshâni: "Initially the metaphysical moment lies in the vacillation of the

 aroused conscience *(nafs-e lawwâma)*[1] between contemplation of the bounty and loving grace of God and the witnessing of the shock of His wrath and rejection — yet realising the excellence of His loving grace and the strength of the soul's yearning for God.

"In the end, the metaphysical moment consists of the heart's achievement of the station of rest, and, despite periods of turbidity, the inception of the station of subsistence in God *(baqâ')*, as the multiple forms of the Essence of Divine Unity begin to display themselves."

RSh, IV, p. 180

2. Abu Sa'id Abe'l-Khair: "Your time is between two breaths: one gone, the next still to come." Then he added, "Yesterday has fled. Where is the morrow? Today is the day."

AT, p. 297

3. Abu Solaimân Dârâni: "Whenever hope prevails over fear, *waqt* goes to waste."

TS (S), p. 76

4. Jonaid: "Lost time cannot be regained. Time is the dearest thing that exists."

TS (S), p. 161

5. Yusef ebn Ḥosain Râzi: "The *faqir* is one who safeguards his 'moment', so if another moment

1. This term is traditionally translated as the 'admonishing soul', or 'blaming self'. The author in his essay "Sufism and Psychoanalysis", *What the Sufis Say* (New York, 1980) describes the blaming self as that aspect of the psyche which "seeks perfection and reproaches the 'commanding self' *(nafs-e ammâreh)* for its passional and animal tendencies." p.29

enters his consciousness while he is engaged in his 'moment' he becomes unworthy of the name, *faqir*.

TS (S), p. 188

6. Ḥallâj: "A man's 'time' is an oyster shell in the ocean of his bosom. Tomorrow, these shells shall be thrown down and shattered on the plain of the Resurrection."

TA, p. 589

7. Abu 'Ali Daqqâq: "Your 'time' is where you are. If you time is in the world, you are worldly. If you are in that of the hereafter, you are of the hereafter. If you are joyous, your time is likewise. If you are aggrived, in 'time', likewise you sorrow."

TA, p. 656

8. Abu Moḥammad 'Abdo'llâh ebn Mobârak: "Your most precious moments are when you are free from the provocation of your passions *(nafs)* and your most blessed hours and moments are those when people harbour no ill-will or suspicion towards you."

RA

9. Shâh Ne'mato'llâh: "Know that time cannot be contained in place. In origin, it consequently belongs to 'beings' and the 'master of time' *(ṣâḥeb-e waqt)* is one being amidst all beings. According to the capacity of the containers, God manifests Himself in the determined forms of possible beings, appearing in a variety of ways, according to the potential of each capacity."

RSh, IV, p. 261

10. Qoshairi: "The meaning of the adage, 'Time is a keen-edged sword' is that whoever handles a sword blade delicately is safe, and whoever handles a blade roughly suffers its wounds. So it is with 'time', whoever submits to its dictates is freed, and whoever abandons resignation to its ordination, resisting it, falls into error.

RQ, p. 90

11. Abu 'Ali Daqqâq: "Time is a file which grinds 'you' down, without causing you to be depreciated in any way; it is liberation through self-eradication and self-annihilation."

RQ, p. 90

12. Abu 'Abdo'llâh Moḥammad ebn Esma'il Maghrebi: "Your most virtuous moments are those spent behaving in harmony *(mowâfeqat)* with people."

RQ, p. 63

13. Qoshairi: "Attention to past time is a misuse of (present) time."

RQ, p. 89

14. Moẓaffar Kermânshâhi: "The most meritorious deed which a devotee may perform is to conserve his time-which is neither falling short nor overstepping the mean in every deed."

RQ, p. 76

15. Abu Sa'id Kharrâz: "Sufism is submission

to time."

TA, p. 462

16. Jonaid: "Sufism is the cherishing of moments."

KST, p. 299

17. Bâbâ Ṭâher: "The *faqir* should not be subject to time. Rather time should be subject to him."

TKQ, p. 579

18. Bâbâ Ṭâher: "If within a *waqt*, the Sufi seeks from God to please himself, it will overwhelm him, prevail upon him, and become his veil. If the Sufi, on the contrary, during such a time pursues the Truth, he himself becomes the veil of time, and subjects it to himself."

TKQ, p. 646

19. Bâbâ Ṭâher: "Until one learns to bear with times *(auqât)* which are superfluous, one will not recognise the reality of time."

TKQ, p. 647

20. Bâbâ Ṭâher: "The states of the mystics who have realised Reality tend to fluctuate among three 'metaphysical moments'. One moment is that in which breath is drawn in to gain some fresh knowledge. Another moment is when that knowledge is generated into reality *(ḥaqiqat)*, and the third is when that reality is transformed into the Truth *(ḥaqq)*. The three degrees of gnosis — the knowledge of certitude *('elm al-yaqin)*, the vision of certitude *('ain al-yaqin)*, and the Truth of certitude

 (ḥaqq al-yaqin) — are implied by this distinction."

TKQ, p. 654

21. Bâbâ Ṭâher: Whoever in a moment's interim, regards the moment alone, fritters away the moment."[1]

TKQ, p. 654

22. Bâbâ Ṭâher: "Cherishing and conserving time is intelligent, but wisdom is in cognisance *(ma'refat)* of time itself."[2]

TKQ, p 655

23. Bâbâ Ṭâher: "Time *(waqt)* spent unoccupied with self, absent from ego-consciousness, is considered gained and profitable, but time spent self-preoccupied is considered wasted and lost."

TKQ, p. 655

24. Ruzbehân: "The metaphysical moment (*waqt)* is between the past and future in the time *(zamân)* of meditation *(morâqeba)*. The appearance of mystical subtleties from the Invisible upon the heart constitutes its reality. Jonaid declared: 'Time is dear, and once lost, is beyond recall."

SS, p. 548

25. Anon: "Time *(waqt)* is the locus of the

1. The creator of time, comments 'Aino'l-Qodhât, should be contemplated, not time alone.
2. One who watches his mystical states, says the same commentator, is clever but one who realises the reality of all states during their fluction is truly wise.

manifestion of creation. It may also be designated by the terms: *ḥâl*[1] and *ân*[2]. The aspirant should be industrious in his vigilance over the means expedient to the metaphysical moment's occurrence, for in bringing together the causes of such moments, he is graced by knowledge *(edrâkât)*, gnostic insight *(ma'âref)*, unveilings of the spirit *(mokâshefât)*, and the contemplative vision *(mo'aiyenât)*."

TT, p. 235

26. Anṣâri: "The Sufi is the 'child of the moment', not the 'child of desire'."

TS(A)

Anṣâri's Conception of Time

From *Pilgrim's Waystations:*

"God declares: 'Then you came hither, O Moses, by My Providence'. *(Qoran*, XX:40).

"*Waqt* is a container, and in this context it has three degrees of meaning:

"First, the moment *(dam)* of true rapture, bringing intimacy with the light of Divine Grace *(faḍhl)* and calling forth the purity of hope in God and the contrition which either provokes true fear of God or arouses the fervour of prayerful yearning *(shauq)* and fans the flames of Divine Love.

"The second meaning of *waqt* concerns the aspirant who pursues his course through (states of) fluctuation and stability, until at last he achieves permanent stability through the focusing of his

[1] See the introduction to Chap.IV.
[2] See the last definition in this chapter.

 states of consciousness *(ḥâl)* and the awareness of knowledge. In one breath, he may be occupied with knowledge, and in another be uplifted by mystical states *(ḥâl)*. While suspended between these two conditions, he is sometimes granted the savour of spiritual delight *(dhauq),* subjecting him to a trial; at other moments Divine Jealousy may veil him and dispersion of consciousness *(tafraqa)* overcome him.

"In its third sense, its meaning is conveyed by the expression: "The present moment is Reality' (*waqt ḥaqq ast)*, alluding to immersion in God at the onset of *waqt*. Such usage, in my opinion, is unwarranted except in the sense that *waqt* be conceived of as an inspiration which strips bare metaphysical intuition *(kashf)* of its theological garb. By this experience, which transcends the ordinary rapture *(wajd)* or ray of vision *(barq)*, the mystic achieves the station of unitive awareness *(jam')* and in settling his accounts *(mo'âmela)* with God, cleanses the fountainhead of his amorous supplication, while his inner being is inebriated with ecstasy."

MS, p. 174

From *One Hundred Battlefields:*

"Metaphysical time (*waqt*) is the ninety-first Battlefield [of spiritual warfare] and arises from the Battlefield of the Instant *(laḥẓa)*. God said: 'You came hither then O Moses, by My Providence'. *Waqt* is exclusve of all other than God. It is experienced in basically three different ways: fleeting and inconstant like a flash of lightning, persistent and fixed, and lastly, overwhelming.

"Time experienced as a flash is purifying in effect, and arises from contemplation *(fekrat)*. It burnishes bright one's reflection upon the hereafter and makes one oblivious to the world.

"Time which persists is aroused by delight in the Divine invocation *(dhekr)*. It keeps one engaged in itself, rather than occupied with the hereafter, until the Truth *(ḥaqq)* becomes evident.

"*Waqt* which overwhelms, kills. It is aroused by the audition of spiritual vision[1]; its appearance eradicates the conditioned habits of the human state, so that the transcendent Truth alone abides."

SM, p. 196

Tahanawi's View of Time

Waqt is something which arbitrarily overwhelms the devotee, such as fear or sorrow or joy, and subjects him to its sway. Hence, the Sufis speak of someone acting according to 'the moment's behest' or say 'time is a keen-edged sword', because by time's onslaught, affairs are cut short.

"In the *Jâme'aṣ-ṣanâye'*, *waqt* is technically defined as a mystical state the arrival of which in the transconsciousness *(serr)* of the devotee bestows tranquillity. It is incumbent upon the gnostic *('aref)* to respond to each moment (*waqt*) appropriately, to meet one moment with gratitude, another with complaint, and another with peace so as to be a true 'child of the moment'. Just as the

1. *as samâ-e naẓar:* This refers to the contemplative vision of the invocation *(tasbiḥ)* of God by all creation. (Author's note)

 child obeys his parents' will, so the gnostic, inwardly and outwardly, is at the beck and call of *waqt*.

"In the commentary on the *Mathnawi* two kinds of Sufis are distinguished. The first type of Sufi is referred to as 'child of the moment' because of his obedient attendance upon time, which masters and subjects him to its sway. The second type is called the 'parent of time' *(abo'l-waqt),* having mastered and sujected time to his own will."

KF, p.1449

'Ezzo'd-Din Maḥmud Kâshâni's Conception of Time

"In the technical terminology of the Sufis, *waqt* possesses the following three meanings:

Waqt is often described as a condition in which the devotee's consciousness becomes subject to states such as contraction *(qabḍh)* and expansion *(basṭ)* or grief *(ḥozn)* and joy *(sorur).* The consciousness of one endowed with such a 'moment' is so overwhelmed and surfeited with mystical feeling *(ḥâl)* that he is incapable of comprehending any other state. One overmastered by contraction, for instance, is so affected by this mood that neither a trace of past nor hint of any future expansion remains. All of his 'times' are tinged with the colour of the state which at the moment he possesses. However, the influence such a person exerts over other people's states is relative to his own state, and this is the source of all errors in his comprehension of the mystical states experienced by those around him. He grants his approbation to those whose states concur with his own and rejects as demented the experience of everyone else. This general sense of the word *waqt*, as expressed in the above exegesis, may apply to both Sufis and non-Sufis.

"Secondly, the term *waqt* is used commonly to denote a mystical state which suddenly appears, as an attack *(hojum)* or onslaught *(mofâjât)* from the Unseen, divesting the aspirant of his individual personality, and making him subservient to its own *modus operandi.* Only the Elect among wayfarers realise this moment, and it is they to whom the masters point, when they say 'the Sufi is the child of the moment'. Furthermore, when characterising someone as being 'at the moment's behest', they refer to the subjection of the the aspirant's desire and will to the Divine decree and volition.

"Whoever refuses to comply with deference and acquiescence to the ordination of the Unseen and proceeds contentiously, becomes subjected to Its wrath. In this light, according to an adage: '*waqt* is a keen-edged sword'[1], a sword being endowed with two qualities: one, softness and pliancy, and the other, keenness and trenchancy. Whoever handles it with softness, and treats it with gentleness, will receive gentleness therefrom. Whoever handles it roughly suffers the wound inflicted by its keen edge. Time, too, has two qualities: gentleness and wrath. Whoever obeys the behest of time willingly, compliantly, enjoys its grace, while whoever willfully strives to inhibit its course, is overcome by its wrath.

"There is a further significance in likening time to a sword: Time is charged to execute the

1. See the author's *Traditions of the Prophet* (New York, 1984) Vol.II p.21 for elucidation of this saying.

Divine Will through all [worldly] designs and [human] states and hence to cleave like a sword in executing its mandate.

"The third significance of *waqt*, however, is the present time or moment *(zamân-e ḥâl)* poised between past and future. Thus when a person is termed 'possessor of time' *(ṣâheb-e waqt)*, it is understood that his endeavour to perform those tasks that are first and foremost in the present moment, inhibits him from preoccupation with the past or anticipation of the future. In other words, he does not 'waste time'.

"Some Sufis, when asked about *waqt,* have indicated that 'it is to contemplate what was allotted one in pre-eternity *(azal)*, and not look forward to what will become of one in post-eternity *(abad)*; and to conscientiously observe God's Will with respect to oneself between breathing in and breathing out'. This kind of *waqt* is not subject to waning or abatement, except with certain way-farers, whose states are tinged with fluctuation *(talwin)*[1]. However, only that period which is spent being present in the moment (*waqt*) do they reckon as part of their lives.

"Once the Sufi has realised 'union-with-God' and a stable spiritual state *(tamkin)*, time becomes eternal to the Sufi, no longer broken by interludes or subject to waning. In the words of Shebli: "My time is eternal and my sea undivided'.

"The master of this 'metaphysical moment' is free from the influence of mystical states. Some Sufis characterise a mystic of this degree as 'father of the moment' rather than 'child of the moment' because he is no longer subject to time (*waqt*) in the second sense and instead, dominates it, using every

1. Literally 'colouration'; its antonym is *tamkin*, which means stability or well-groundedness of spiritual state.

moment wisely and to its utmost."

MH, p. 138

Ruzbehân's Vision of Time

"When freed at last from passing through the spiritual stations, the King of Love inaugurates the heart's work, stirring the Sufi on to realize the vision of Love's majesty. No material pleasures are left to the heart, which has become a mirror of the Angelic Pleroma *(malakut)*. The lights of the realm of Divine Ordainment *(jabarut)* are displayed to his heart, which is enraptured in nearness to God. His mystical state is steadfast between absence [from God] *(ghaibat)*, presence [with God] *(ḥoḍhur)*, obliteration [of self] *(maḥw)*, and sobriety *(ṣaḥw)*.[1]

"Lightning rays of revelation now blaze forth from the cloud of the Invisible, while from the firmament of Eternity a shower of inspiration pours down upon the earth of the heart, whereon flowers of spiritual longing *(shauq)* spring up. The mystic's transconscious self *(serr)* is stirred from the ground of human nature *(fetrat)* towards its Divinely hallowed source, as the spirit's brightness is overwhelmed by the dazzling glory of contemplation while transfixed in bewildered rapture *(hairat)*. In this state the Sufi is said to be in the station of *waqt*. As long as these conditions prevail, gnostics consider him to be a 'possessor of *waqt*'.

1. Elsewhere in this same treatise, Ruzbehân defines sobriety as the "maintenance of knowledge during the contemplation of God in intoxication and ecstasy." For a detailed discussion see the author's *Sufism: Fear and Hope... Annihilation and Subsistence* (New York, 1982) pp.75-85. The author's Persian language text: *Ma'âref-e ṣufiya*. (London: 1983), Vol. II, provides the detailed description of the three previous terms.

"The significance of *waqt* is in the theophany of subtle spiritual truths *(ḥaqâ'eq)*, which from the realm of the Invisible appear to the eye of the spirit dressed in the garb of interior revelations *(kashf)*. Once the sweetness of these interior revelations have purged the spirit (which at this point, is divested of its formal limitations and stands outside of itself) one is said to be 'within metaphysical time' *(dar waqt)*. In the theophany revealed to Moses, do you not see a sign of this?

And when his Lord revealed Himself to the mountain,
He shattered it to dust, and Moses
fell down senseless.[1]

"The gnostic's inward contemplation of Truth can no longer be interrupted by temporal events during this time. No created being intrudes in his heart; all stray thoughts are effaced, and even the instants *(laḥẓat)* vanish. Similarly, the Prophet of God typified his own metaphysical moment as severing his God-graced heart from all but the Truth, as it delighted in the Beatific Vision. 'I have a time with God', he said, 'that no archangel or previous prophet can share with me'.[2]

"His meaning was: 'whenever I come near the bright carrier of Pre-Eternity's vision, neither archangels nor prophets, no Throne, nor heavens, nor earth, can endure my presence, because of the awe-inspring Trust with which Eternity enfolds my heart. There I am in the station of unification *(etteḥâd)*. Nothing created, nothing tainted by

1. Qoran VII, 142: Arberry, *Koran Interpreted*, slightly modified.
2. See the author's *Traditions of the Prophet*, Vol. I, (New York, 1981) p.31

being, can bear with me. In this state, one hair of mine is more weighty than both the Throne and the Pedestal'.

"Know that *waqt* is particular to the gnostic or knower *('aref)*, rather than the Known *(ma'ruf)*, Whose Transcendence surpasses all appearance and disappearance, all time and place. The veil of His Majesty and Grandeur He draws close or lifts from the eyes of the knower as He wills. Here neither day nor night exist: 'With God, there is no day and night'. What is presented here, however, is only a small fragment of the principles of Divine Unity, so let this not become a cause of error for those who have never realised any vision of the Transcendent.

"If the radiation of the lights of spiritual truths is sustained, the gnostic's time (*waqt*) will become continuous, bringing attainment of stability in pure remembrance *(dhekr)* of God, where the gnostic comes to savour the relish of mystical feeling *(ḥâl)*. Though the ardour of his intoxication *(sokr)*[1] may diminish, the purity of his *waqt* is not decreased. His state resembles that of Shebli, who described his moments *(auqât)* to his disciples as follows: 'Your metaphysical moment is all bits and pieces, but mine is indivisible and ever-present'; and then he added, 'my moment is eternal *(sarmad)*, ever-flowing, without any break'. He implied by saying this, that the state granted him by God was endless and unceasing, by grace of the purity of his veneration of God, the sincerity of his invocation of God, the ardour of his yearning heart, and his detachment from all things for God's sake. That which is endless and infinite, it follows, is also eternal. God says:

1. See the author's *Sufism: Fear and Hope...* Chap. IV, for the explanation of this term.

If the sea were ink
For the Words of my Lord
The sea would be spent
Before the Words of my Lord are spent.[1]

"The words of God have no end because their Bestower is infinite. As someone else has said, 'Whoever knows God, loves Him, and whoever loves Him, drowns in a sea of sorrow'. *Waqt* is defined by one gnostic as 'the perpetuation of visionary perception in the heart, relative to different types of ecstatic dispositions *(mawâjed).*

MA, pp.81-82

Lines by Jâmi on Time

Waqt they say, is
a keen-edged blade
because it unceasingly
cleaves the seconds.

Wherever it flies
neither cries nor sighs
arrest the advance
of its blade.

Time's track is just a breath, yet
its influence immense, its mint imprinted
for aeons on the heart.

Try to make its transpiration
match your soul's aspiration;
Strive to preserve time's trace,
to hold its mark within the soul.

1. *Qoran* XVIII, 110; Arberry, *op. cit.*, slightly modified.

Time is a metaphysical blade
made to slay foes —
a shame then that it should dismember
friends
when its point was made for foes!

What 'foes' though?
the enemies of consciousness.
What is consciousness?
God awareness;
its foes: the appetites and *anima bruta*.[1]

HA, p. 35

Time Acording to Shâh Ne'mato'llâh

Know that metaphysical time *(waqt)* is the very duration in which you are, at the present moment.[2] It is a condition of being *(amr-e wojudi)* interposed between two non-beings. According to an Arabic proverb, '*Waqt* is a condition, the prevailing power of which restrains one from attending to all other matters.' Each person experiences contraction *(qabḍh)*, expansion *(basṭ)*, grief *(ḥozn)* and gladness *(sorur)*, according to his or her spiritual aptitude. God declares:

"....And He gives you all you ask Him for;"
(XIV: 33)

— the interpretation of this being that every affair of Divinity *(sh'un-e ḥaqq)* for which you ask God, will be granted you precisely as befits your spiritual

1. *nafs*
2. Literally translated, '*Waqt* is the present time in which you are in'.

 aptitude. God declares:

"Every day He is engaged in another affair *(sha'n)*"

(LV: 29)[1]

Indeed, through the archetypes *(a'yân)* of possible beings, God directs His orders, and despite His foreordainment of all possibilities, His mandate is issued to the inherent capacities *(emkân)* and intuitive faculties *(adhwâq)* of the darvishes in their contemplative moments.

Yet if a wayfarer should happen to fall into the sea of heart-contraction *(qabḍh)*, he must abandon himself to its waves, until he should reach the shore once again. If, instead, he chooses to flail his hands and feet about, his contraction will only increase with every breath, and at every instant *(laḥẓ')* his *waqt* will be wrested away from him.

RSh, IV, p. 261

'Instant' *(ân)*

In the terminology of the Sufis, the word, 'instant' *(ân;* plural: *awân)* denotes the very time *(waqt)* in which you exist. 'Instant' cannot be contained in any place.[2] It is gnosis *(ma'refat)*. It cannot be modified by an article, because it does not admit of any partnership.

TJ, p. 35

1. The previous line before this sentence provides clarification: "Whatsoever is in Heaven and Earth ask of Him".
2. Literally, 'The moment is a vessel without location'.

نَفَس

VII

Breath

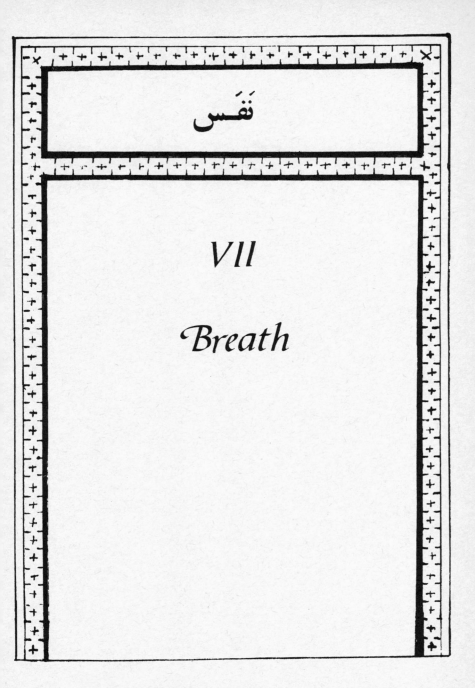

PART 1

The Arabic Term for Breath *(Nafas)*

Tell my beloved, my heart-holder
O Breath of Dawn:
How all my doings are snarled like the dawn
on a breath.

— Sa'di

In the *Alchemy of Happiness (Kimiyâ-ye sa'âdat),* Abu Ḥamed Ghazâli provides the following explanation of *nàfas:*

"Breath in its literal significance, refers to the inhalation of air through the nose or mouth in order to pacify the heart, and the subsequent diffusion of vapour through the same passageway. This combined avtivity of inspiration and expiration constitutes one breath.

"Breath is a jewel, figuratively speaking, the value of which constitutes the very substance of man, and wasteful expenditure of which is folly."

"Each breath inspired", Sa'di tells us, "is the fosterer of life, and every breath expired brings elation to the spirit."[1]

"As a technical term in Sufism," explains Qoshairi, "breath is the administering of consolation to the heart through subtleties from the realm of the Invisible *(latâ'ef-e ghoyub).* The character of

1. G, p.4

one who ‘possesses’ breath, however, is kindlier and simpler than that of one who is a ‘possessor’ of mystical states. According to the Sufis, one who ‘possesses’ breath *(ṣaḥeb-e nafas)* is an adept, and one who is a ‘possessor’ of time *(ṣaḥeb-e waqt)* is a beginner, while the ‘possessor’ of mystical states *(saheb-e hâl)* holds a rank intermediary between the two. Mystical states are but a means, intermediary on advancement. The people of heart are concerned with metaphysical time; the initiates of the spirit with mystical states, while breath is the affair of adepts of the transconscious self *(ahl-e sarâ‘er).*”

RQ, p. 127

The Sense and Syntax of *Breath (nafas)* in Sufism

1. One meaning which *nafas* may evoke is that of a supplication or entreaty for Divine succour. Neẓâmi employs this term in this sense in one of his verses:

Souls were consoled by his breath;
Lips were sealed by his words.

It is with this meaning in mind that Sa‘di remarks, ‘Thanks to the auspicious example of the darvishes and their edifying inspiration *(ṣedq-e nafas)* a blameworthy character is transmuted into a virtuous disposition.’

G, p. 186

2. ‘To breath’ or ‘breathing’ among the Sufis quite often means simply ‘to inspire’ with spiritual

fervour. Beginners in the initial stages of their spiritual and ethical development *(sair wa soluk)* on the path have this sense in mind when they appeal to the support *(hemmat)* of the Sufi master to aid and inspire their efforts. 'O Master!' they may implore, 'favour me with a breath!' — Hence, simple Persian expressions such as, 'The Master breathed', *(pir nafas kard)* imply that 'The Master lent the grace of his inspiration'.

3. The Breath of Truth *(nafas-e ḥaqq)*

Utterance of this expression is rooted in another Sufi belief. Since God is understood to be everywhere, visible and audible for all who are attuned, no word, no sound is considered devoid of Divine Wisdom. With this faith, Sufis strive to hear the Divine word in all things. Hence an idiom such as, 'Yours is the very breath of Truth', *(nafasat-e ḥaqq ast),* implying by extension that, 'Your words are a Divine inspiration', has come into usage among the Sufis. This phrase usually takes the form of a reply to the Sufi Master, or a fellow disciple. Its use furthermore acknowledges the Sufi's understanding of the Divine inspiration, rather than mere human opinion, contained in a Master's statements. 'Your breath is the very Truth', hence implies, 'Your words demand my respectful obedience!'

4. The Master of Breath *(ṣâḥeb-e nafas)*

This expression is used as an honorary epithet for the saint or master who causes events to occur as he determines or declares. In theological terms, his prayers are answered.

5. The Messiah-like Breath.

This idiom serves as a metaphor for the

quickening a master's breath may have on souls which have become moribund and overmastered by their passions, as in this example from Ḥâfeẓ:

> Be cheerful, my heart — I sense it in the air;
> Someone's inspiration on the way —
> a blissful breath,
> a Messiah-like inspiration.

6. Awareness of Breath *(wâqef-e nafas budan)*

This idiom alludes to the Sufis' practice of constantly taking cognisance of God, of checking themselves lest any breath escape in unconsciousness of the Beloved. Jâmi faithfully reflects this meaning in his *Flashes (Lawâ'eḥ,* p.60):

> Whether active or still, one should be present in the moment *(waqt)*, heedful lest a single second of one's life should expire in vain. One must observe one's breath. Let no exhalation escape oblivious.

7. The Breath of the Divine Mercy *(nafas-e raḥmân)*[1]

This term is endowed with a distinctive significance in Sufi theosophical thought. Abdo'r-Razzâq Kâshâni writes:

"The breath of the Divine Mercy or Clemency *(nafas-e raḥmâni)* is relative being *(wojud-e eḍhâfi)*, which is one in reality, but multiple in its appearance in the archetypal forms *(ṣowar-e ma'âni)*, that is to say, in the permanent archetypes

1. In the translation of this section much of the terminology employed in Izutsu's definitive study: *A Comparative Study of the Key Philosophical Concepts in Sufism and Taoism*, Part One (Tokyo, 1967) p.127ff, has been adopted. For a detailed treatment of this term, see also Ebn 'Arabi's *Fusus al-Hikam*, tr. from Arabic to French by T. Burckhart, and from French to English by A. Culme-Seymour, as *The Wisdom of the Prophets* (London, 1975) pp. 73-82, 89-90.

(a'yân) and their concrete aspects *(aḥkâm)* on the plane of the Divine Unicity *(wâḥediyat)*. Human breath is multiple in a similar manner in dilation and division into sound-forms or letters *(ṣowar-e ḥoruf)*. Just as human respiration is constituted of an emission of warm air from within, with the repulsion of cold air, bringing relief to the breather, likewise the spiritual principle of breath represents the dilation and consequent consolation of the Divine Names, which are encompassed by the Name *ar-Raḥmân* (the Merciful).

All-Being appeared in a breath expired,
articulated in the dilation of the true dawn,
bursting open the gates
of this cosmic abode.

RSh, IV, p.80

In his *Tract On Guidance (Resâla-ye hedâyat)* Shâh Ne'mato'llâh explains 'the Breath of the Divine Mercy' in the following manner:

"The Breath of the Divine Mercy is an existential self-manifestation *(tajalli-ye wojudi)*[1] apparent on the level of Divinity. Although the theophany *(maẓhar)* of the Greatest Name *(esm-e a'ẓam)* is itself the Greatest Name, the Breath of Divine Mercy is designated as analogous to the level of Divinity, as it bears within itself all the concrete aspects of the Divine Names, which are the universal archetypes *(ṣurat-e kolliyya)* of the level of Divinity. The first visible effect of the

1. According to Ebn 'Arabi, the emanation, or self-manifestation of Divinity, has two phases: first, the *(tajalliyo'l-aqdas)*, the 'most holy emanation' of Unity on the plane of Unicity *(wâhediyyah)* and secondly, the emanation of Oneness into manyness, into the world, i.e. an 'existential *(wojudi)* emanation'. Cf. Izutsu, *op.cit.*, pp.145-8.

 Breath of Divine Mercy appears by the grace of the Comprehensive Name, *Allâh*. Subsequent effects are determined by the Universal Names, such as *al-Raḥman* (the Merciful), then by Subordinate Names *(asma'-e tâlliya)*, and lastly, by Particular Names *(asma'-e joziyah)* which generate the archetypal essences *(a'yân)* of individual beings."

RSh, II, p. 190

The anonymous author of the *Mirror of Lovers (Mer'ât-e 'oshâq)*, an undated manual of Sufi mystical terminology, speaks of this term as follows:

"It is the perpetual outpouring, or effusion *(faiḍh)*, of Being upon the created essences. Such an effusion is unitary and one if viewed from its wellspring in the Divine Unity, from whence it is likened to that dilation of breath which in human respiration serves to relieve the 'animal spirit' *(ruḥ-e ḥaiwâni)*. It is multiple, however, if viewed in its connection to relative beings *(wojudât-e eḍhâfi)*, from whence it is analogous to the multiplicity of human breaths discharged into sound-forms, or 'letters' *(ḥoruf)*."

TT, p. 233

Another term employed by the Sufis is the 'perpetuation of the breath of the Divine Mercy' *(emtedâd-e nafas Raḥmâni)*. The above author comments:

"[This expression] designates the perpetual irradiation *(tajalli)* of the Divine Essence[1] upon all the deployed aspects *(makhârej)* of the levels

1. Cf. T. Burckhard's *Introduction to Sufi Doctrine* (tr. D.M.Matheson, Wellingborough, 1976) p.76.

(marâteb) of transcendant configurations *(ḥoruf-e 'âliya)*[1], the perfections of being, and the 'complete carriers' *(marâkebât-e tâmma)*[2] of phenomena. This irradiation comprises the manifestation of the hypostatic orders of Being *(sho'unât),* the appearance of Divine Grace, and all possible beings. Hence, the Tradition (of the Prophet): 'The breath of the Divine Mercy comes to me from Yemen'."[3]

TT, p. 172

8. 'Breath-friend' *(ham-nafas)*[4]

This expression designates a faithful and intimate friend, a confidant of sympathetic disposition on the Way. Its usage is exemplified in a celebrated *robâ'i* by 'Erâqi:

The world's a breath
the *amor* of lovers, the Beloved Herself
    just a breath,
So, go and find
your breathfriend, your anima-conspirator—
    the world's a breath,
Sit a second's breath
side by side with a friend
in breath — behold your collected lifespan
    just a breath.

1. i.e. the determined forms, or permanent archetypes *(a'yân ath-thâbeta)*
2. i.e. the intelligible receptacles of possibilities.
3. See A. Schimmel's *Mystical Dimension of Islam* (North Carolina, USA, 1975), p. 25, for further commentary on this tradition.
4. The Persian term *ham-dam* as well as this Perso-Arabic term are both almost exactly equivalent to the Latin: *conspiratio: a blowing* or *breathing together*. Hence: *harmony, agreement, union.* Unfortunately only the negative sense of the word: *conspiracy,* is reflected in its usage in modern English.

Words of the Masters on Breath

"Sufis have said: 'The most pious act of devotion is numbering one's breaths before God Almighty.' Furthermore, they say that first God created the hearts, making them the fountainhead of His gnosis. Subsequently, He created the hidden centres of transconsciousness *(asrâr)*, which he designed as the locus of Divine Unity *(tauḥid)*.[1] Hence every breath not drawn with a view to gaining spiritual cognition *(ma'refat)* and with reference to Unity, is lifeless, wherefore its owner will be held responsible'.

"I have heard Abu 'Ali Daqqâq say: 'The gnostic need not possess breath, being incapable of any culpable negligence, but the lover must resort to breath, or else he will perish from impatience'."

RQ, p. 128

Anṣâri's Conception of Breath

From *Pilgrims Waystations:*

God declares, "When Moses awoke, he cried: 'Glory be to God'."[2]

The word *nafas* (breath) is derived from the Arabic root *n-f-s* (meaning: 'to console, 'appease', 'relieve', or 'dilate').

'Breath' has three levels, analogous to different degrees of 'metaphysical time'.

The first level transpires amidst darkness and

1. Concerning the antiquity of this myth, see Schimmel, *op. cit.*, p.192
2. This exclamation of Moses in the Qoran (VII:143) follows his vision of God upon a mountain.

concealment, containing suppressed rage, and pertaining to knowledge. The breath and respiration of anyone affected by this condition is filled with sighs and regret, while brusqueness is evident in their speech. These effects are produced, in my view, by the estrangement of their gloomy and shrouded condition, which is termed the 'station of darkness'.

'Breath' on the second level, transpires during illumination *(tajalli),* ascending from the station of elation or rejoicing *(sorur)* towards the solace of contemplative vision *(mo'âyena)*[1]. Surfeited with the light of Being, this breath bestows discrimination at the point where allusions are cut off.

The third level of breath is consecrated with the water of sanctity. It is an oyster shell of light, subsistent through the dispensation of Pre-eternity.

For one of a zealous character the first breath is a lamplight. For the determined seeker, the second breath is a means of mystical ascension. The third breath is a royal crown for adepts.

MS, pp. 181-3

From *One Hundred Battlefields:*

Breath *(nafas)* is the ninety-second battlefield (of spiritual combat) and arises from the battlefield of metaphysical time.

God said, "When Moses awoke, he cried, 'Glory be to God'."

The breath of the master of metaphysical time is free of all outward tarnish. Adepts in reality have

1. *Mo'âyena* constitutes number ninety-eight of Anṣâri's *Hundred Battlefields (of Spiritual Combat) (Ṣad maidân).*

 three breaths:

1. A sweet plaint.
2. An infatuated cry.
3. A shout of ecstasy.

The sweet plaint dispels demons, absolves all sin, and opens the heart.

The infatuated cry purges one of love for the world, sweeps material casuality away, and causes one to be oblivious of people *(khalq)*.[1]

The shout of ecstasy pierces the soul, sets the heart athirst and burns away the veils.

SM, p.198

Ruzbehân on Breath

"Breaths are perfumed breezes, each one of which is borne upon the *Boreas* of amorous intimacy, diffusing a revelation of the Divine Essence and Qualities, redolent with the scents of the gardens of the realms of the Invisible and the Invisible of the Invisible, conveying the most precious of arcane knowledge, and fraught with an ecstatic vision of time without beginning and end.

"God declares: 'I swear by the breath of the morning' (LXXXI, 18). In the words of one gnostic, 'Breath is the blowing of the Divine upon censers of the Holy Spirit, which scatter forth gentle breezes of Divine Union, bearing the fragrance of the Divine Beauty."

MA, p.199

1. Or 'creation'. The term 'infatuated cry' *(na'ra-ye wâjed)* usually describes the love-lorn wailing of the Sufis during *Samâ*, affected by an ecstatic state *(ḥâl)* or moved by rapture *(wajd)*.

“Breath is that which rises from the heart accompanied by the invocation of God *(dhikr)*, its truth aflame with the Divine manifestaion *(tajalli)*, issuing through the mouth of the Spirit. The possessor of breath is vigilantly observative of his visionary experiences *(moshâhedat)*, rebutting delusive fantasies *(waswâs)* by taking account of his breaths.”

SS, p.565

According to ‘Abdo’r-Razzâq Kâshâni’s description, “breath provides consolation to the heart through [animation of] the realities of the subtle world. Breath is the intimacy of the lover and the Beloved.”

Shâh Ne‘mato’llâh’s poetic commentary upon the above sentence follows:

If the Real Object of the lover’s entente
With the Beloved be accounted a breath,
In love let their breaths unite, conspire as one
Until the Beloved becomes the breath he breathes.

RSh, IV, p.80

To conclude, Jâmi writes:

“I quote my price as just a breath;”
said a gnostic firm-set in faith,
“I neither glance back, nor look ahead;
My whole business is founded on breath.”

HA, p. 33

The Persian Term for Breath *(Dam)*[1]

Ah! sighs the breath in; *hu* suspires out
As if to say
in every breath: hullaballo!

Sabzewâri, *Diwân*

The word *dam* like *nafas,* is used as a technical term among the Sufis in Persian to mean 'breath'. Quite often it is synonmous with the idiom, 'gentle Divine breeze' *(nafḥa-ye elâhi),* which is more or less equivalent to the aforementioned 'breath of the Divine Mercy'.

'Dam' as Synonymous with *'Nafas'*

In the following verse by Ḥâfeẓ, the usage of *dam* is equivalent to *nafas:*

The doctor of *Amor* is empathetic,
endowed with the breath *(dam)* of Jesus,
but what worth are his palliatives
if you have no pain?

Dam is most often used to characterise masters, saints or Sufis whose inner nature is purified, their breath giving life to those 'souls' who are dead through being subjected to their selfish passions *(nafs)*, and perfecting those who are

1. The etymological root of *dam,* a native Persian word, is Indo-European, cognate with the Sanskrit *tan,* meaning duration; the Latin *tempus* (time) and *tendere* (to stretch) are derived from the same root, and correspondingly, the English 'time' and 'tension'. *Dam* is synonymous in classical (and modern) Persian with the Arabic *nafas,* when it is applied in the sense, not of time, but of 'breath'.

imperfect. With this in mind, 'Aṭṭâr says:

As 'Aṭṭâr's words give life to the soul
Clearly he is of the same breath as Jesus.

The Designation of *'Dam'* as 'the Breath of the Divine Mercy' or 'a Divine Breeze'

The origin of this peculiar technical connotation of *dam* derives from the saying of the Prophet, 'Divine breezes from your Lord waft through the days of your life. Listen! Be aware of them."[1]

Rumi writes:

The Prophet said,
"Fragrant spiritual breezes are on the wing
from your Lord through the course of your days...
Beware of these moments,
and catch them as they fly.
A zephyr springs up, sees you and flees.
bestows its grace on whom it pleases,
then passes on.
Beware lest another pass by,
find you heedless, leave you standing.
The soul on fire is quenched by this breeze;
the moribund soul is quickened into motion —
A heaven-sent motion, subtle and sublime,
nothing like the motion of created things.
Were this wind driven down on heaven and earth,
they would balk from bearing its charge.

1. A reference to the *Qoran:* XXXIII, 72: "Lo! We offered the trust to the heavens and the earth and the mountains, but they shrank from it and were afraid of it. And man assumed it. Lo! he hath proved a tyrant and a fool!" (Pickthall's translation, slightly modified)

Through dread of this self-same boundless breath
take note: "they shrank from bearing" the trust,
since they "were afraid of it"
how harrowed the mountain's blood turned to water
aghast at such a mighty charge.

MM, II: 1951-59

'Aṭṭâr writes:

If the wellspring of everything were not that breath,
neither man nor world would exist.

Maghrebi writes:

Morningtide, your ruby lips sighed
over non-being's kingdom a breath —
In one breath, you gave this world birth.

Of this expression, Sanâ'i writes:

Adam's father on earth was the breath
borne by Mary;
The flesh was imbued with Adam's hue
The soul was formed of the breath's scent
Natives of this breath are all Adam, all men
Aliens to this breath are all blank canvases,
hollow men.

HH, p. 185

Idioms Relating to *'Dam'* in the Sufi Lexicon

1. 'The warm breath' *(dam-e garm)*

It is traditional in a Sufi gathering for a master or attending darvishes to express their appreciation to a singer of Sufi poetry whose harmonious and inspired voice induces states of rapture and ecstasy in those present with the phrase, 'You have a warm breath', which implies, 'How heartfelt, how full of fervour is your voice.'

2. The 'breath of men' *(dam-e mardom)*

This expression alludes to Sufi masters.

3. The 'friend-in-breath' *(ham-dam)*[1]

This expression indicates an intimate friend of like temper and a companion on the Way.

4. The 'blessed breath' *(mobârak dam)*

This expression signifies the inspired breath of the saints of God.

There is someone of blessed breath in this city,
whose piety is possessed by few.

Anon.

5. 'Breath is a Godsend' or 'The present moment is precious' *(dam ghanimat ast)*.

This expression, prevalent among the Sufis, draws attention to the profound significance of every breath or every moment. A breath passed is

1. See page 107; note four.

 a breath perished and, hence, irredeemable. Each breath or moment should be used to its maximum potential. Sa'di in this sense advises:

Treasure, my friend,
the Christ-inspired breath
of the dawn-break;
Perchance
this God-sent breeze may
quicken your love-dead heart.

And Ḥâfeẓ admonishes us:

Treasure the moment,
O heart!
Life's entire legacy,
if you but knew,
is a breath.

6. The 'cold breath' *(dam-e sard)*

This expression is the opposite of the 'warm breath'. It is used to characterise anyone whose words lack any heartfelt enthusiasm and whose speech is cold and uninspired. Public preachers, as well as fanatics full of sanctimonious advice, are generally characterised as having 'cold breath' by the Sufis. After this fashion, Ẓohuri says:

Do not feel numbed or flustered if public preachers
are cold breathed;
You drink wine.
God is kind.

7. 'Breath and smoke' *(dam va dud)*

This idiom was employed traditionally in Sufi

khânaqâhs,[1] where the kindling of fires on the hearth, the cooking of food for the Sufis, the preparation and service of tea, and the singing of mystical poems, were all described as 'breath and smoke'. 'Smoke' in this case referred to the smoke of the kitchen hearth and the charcoal burners on which the tea and coffee pots were steeped. The 'breath' referred to the singing of Sufi poetry and the boiling of food-kettles.

8. 'Singing in chorus' *(dam gereftan)*

It is customary in Sufi gatherings for a singer to sing a poem, and at specified intervals between every few lines, the Sufis join in to chant the refrain, either an invocation or a verse of poetry. This term literally means, 'to breathe in unison', figuratively connoting 'singing in chorus'.

1. The meeting house of the Sufis. See the author's essay: 'The Rules and Manners of the Khânaqâh', *In the Tavern of Ruin* (New York, 1978), pp. 65-88

BIBLIOGRAPHY

Aflâki, Shamso'd-Din Aḥmad. *Manâqeb al-ârefin.* 2 vols., Ankara, 1959-61. In Persian.

Aḥsâ'i,Mohammad ebn Abi Jomhur. *Mojli.* Edited by Aḥmad Shirâzi. Tehran, n.d. In Arabic.

Anṣâri, Khwâja 'Abdo'llâh. *Majmo'a-ye Resa'il Khwâja 'Abdo'llâh Anṣâri.* Edited by Waḥid Dastgerdi. 2nd edition, Tehran, 1968. In Persian.

———. *Manâzel as.-sâ'irin.* Arabic text edited by S. Laugier de Beaurecueil, reprinted with introduction, notes, and Persian translations of the *Elal al-maqâmat* and the *Manazel as-sâ'irin* by Ravân Farhadi. *Ṣad maidan* and sections of the *Tafsir* are printed as commentary beside the *Manâzel as-sâ'irin.* Kabul, 1976.

———. and Ebn 'Ata'illah. *Intimate Conversations/ The Book of Wisdom.* Anṣari's *Monâjat,* translated by Wheeler Thackston, and Ebn 'Ata' illâh's *Kitâb al-hikam* translated by Victor Danner. London, 1978.

———. *Resa'il Khwâja 'Abdo'llâh Anṣâri.* Edited by Moḥammad Shirwani. Tehran, 1963. In Persian.

———. *Ṣad maidân.* Edited by Qâsem Anṣâri. Tehran, 1979. In Persian.

———. *Tafsir-e 'erfani va âdabi-ye Qor'ân-e majid.* Edited by Ḥabibo'llâh Amuzegâr. Tehran, 1969. In Persian.

———. *Ṭabaqât as-ṣufiyyah.* Edited by 'Abdo'l-Ḥaiy Ḥabibi. Kabul, 1968. In Persian.

Arberry, A.J., trans. *Muslim Saints and Mystics.* London, 1976. Partial translation of Aṭṭâr's *Tadhkerat al-auliyâ.*

_____.*The Doctrine of the Sufis.* Partial translation of Kalâbadhi's *Kitâb at-ta'arruf.* Cambridge, 1977.

_____.*The Koran Interpreted.* Oxford University Press, 1983.

Aṭṭar, Farido'd-Din. *Asrâr-nâma.* Edited by Seyyed Ṣâdeq Gauharin. Tehran, 1959. In Persian.

_____.*Diwan-e qasâ'ed wa tarji'ât wa ghazaliyât.* Edited by Sa'id Nafisi. Tehran, 1960. In Persian.

_____.*Oshtor-nâma.* Edited by Mahdi Mohaqqeq. Tehran, 1960. In Persian,

_____.*Tadhkerat al-auliyâ.* Edited by Mohammad Este'lâmi. Tehran, 1975. In Persian.

Bâba Ṭâher 'Oriyan. *Sharḥ-e aḥwâl wa âthâr wa do-baitihâye Bâbâ Ṭâher* (including the: *Sharḥ wa tarjoma'ye kalamât-e qeṣâr* ascribed to 'Aino 1-Qodhât Hamadâni.) Edited by Javâd Maqsur. Tehran, 1975. Persian and Arabic texts.

Bâkhrazi, Abo'l-Mofâkher. *Aurâd al-aḥbâb wa fosus al-âdâb.* Edited by Iraj Afshâr. Vol. 2, Tehran, 1979. In Persian.

Bertels, Yevgeni Edvardovich. *Taṣawwof wa adabiyât-e taṣawwof.* Translated from Russian into Persian by Sirus Izadi. Tehran, 1977. Includes the anonymous glossary of Persian Sufi terminology: the *Mer'ât-e 'oshâq.* Tehran, 1977.

Corbin, Henri. *The Man of Light in Iranian Sufism.* Translated into English from the French by Nancy Pearson. London, 1982.

'Erâqi, Fakhro'd-Din Ebrâhim. *Kolliyât 'Erâqi.* Edited by Sa'id Nafisi. Tehran, 1959. In Persian.

_____.*Resâla-ye lama'ât wa resâla-ye eṣṭelâḥât.* Edited by Dr. Javâd Nurbakhsh. Tehran, 1974. In Persian.

Ghazâli, Abu Ḥamed Moḥammad. *Eḥyâ-ye 'olom-e din.* Translated from Arabic to Persian by Mo'ayyedo'd -Din Moḥammad Khwârazmi and edited by Ḥosain Khadiw Jam. Tehran, 1981, 8 volumes.

_____.*Kimiyâ-ye sa'âdat.* Edited by Aḥmad Arâm. Tehran, 1954. In Persian.

Ḥâfeẓ, Shamso'd-Din Moḥammad. *Diwân.* Edited by Nazir Aḥmad and Reza Jalâli Na'ini. Tehran, 1976.

In Persian.

Hojwiri, ‘Ali ebn ‘Othmân. *Kashf al-maḥjub.* Persian text edited by V.A. Zhukovsky. Leningrad, 1926. English translation by R.A. Nicholson under the above title (from an incomplete M.S): London, 1976. References to Zhukovsky's edition are indicated by: ‘KM (orig.)’ and to Nicholson's translation by: ‘KM (trans.)’, throughout this book.

Izutsu, Toshihiko. *A Comparative Study of the Key Philosophical Concepts of Sufism and Taoism.* 2 vols. Tokyo, 1966-7.

Jami, ‘Abdo'r-Rahmân. *Haft aurang.* Edited by Morteḍhâ Gilani. Tehran, 1978. In Persian.

Lawâ'eḥ. Persian text edited and translated into French by Yann Richard, *Les Jaillissements de Lumiere,* Paris, 1982.

——.*Nafaḥât al-ons.* Edited by Mehdi Tuhidipur. Tehran, 1964. In Persian.

Jorjâni, ‘Ali ebn Moḥammad al-. *at-Ta'rifât.* Edited by Gustavus Fluegel. Lipsiae, 1845. In Arabic.

Kalâbâdhi, Abu Bakr Mohammad. *Al-ta'arrof li-madhab ahl at-taṣawwof.* A. J. Arberry has made an abbreviated English translation from the Arabic of this text: *The Doctrine of the Sufis* (Cambridge, 1977). However the citations in this book refer solely to the *Kholâsa-ye sharḥ-e ta'arrof,* edited by Aḥmad ‘Ali Raja i, Tehran, 1970, which is an abbreviation in Persian by an anonymous writer of the celebrated *Commentary on the Ta'arrof (Sharḥ-e ta'arrof)* being a Persian translation and exegesis of Kâlabadhi's opus by Moḥammad ebn ‘Abdo'llâh Mostamli Bokhârâ'i.

Kâshâni, ‘Abdo'l-Razzâq. *Eṣṭelâḥât aṣ-ṣufiyyah.* Edited by Moḥammad Kamâl Ebrâhim Ja‘far. Egypt, 1981. In Arabic. A partial Persian translation of, and versified commentary upon this work was made by Shah Ne‘mato'llâh in the fourth volume of his *Collected Treatises* (see listing under Shah Ne‘mato'llâh).

Kạshâni, ‘Ezzo'd-Din Mahmud. *Meṣbâḥ al-hedâyah.*

Edited by Jalâlo' d-Din Homâ'i. Tehran, 1946. In Persian.

Kharaqâni, Shaikh Abo'l-Ḥasan. *Aḥwâl wa aqwâl Shaikh Abo'l-Ḥasan Kharaqâni* (including: *Montakhab-e nuro'l-'olum.)* Edited by Mojtaba Minuvi. Tehran, 1980. In Persian.

Kobra, Najmo d-Din *Fawayeḥ al-jamâl wa fawateḥ al-jalâl.* Edited by Fritz Meier. Weisbaden, 1957. In Arabic.

Loṭfo'llâh, Moḥammad ebn Abo'r-Ruh. *Ḥâlât wa sokhanan-e Abu Sa'id Abe' l-Khair.* Tehran, 1952. In Persian.

Maghrebi, Moḥammad Sherin. *Diwan-e Kâmel-e Shams-e Maghrebi* (including: *Resala-ye jam-e jahân-namâ).* Edited with an introduction by Abu Tâleb Mir 'Abedini. Tehran, 1979. In Persian.

Monawar, Moḥammad ebn al-. *Asrar at-tauḥid fi maqâmât as-Shaikh Abu-Sa'id.* Edited by Dhabiho'llâh Ṣafâ. Fifth reprint, Tehran, 1982. In Persian.

Nasafi, 'Azizo'd-Din. *Ketab al-ensân al-kâmel.* Edited by Marijan Molé. Tehran and Paris, 1962. In Persian.

Nurbakhsh, Dr. Javad. *Sufism: Fear and Hope, Contraction and Expansion, Gathering and Dispersion, Intoxication and Sobriety, Annihilation and Subsistance.* New York, 1982.

———. *Traditions of the Prophet (Aḥâdith).* Vol. 1. New York, 1981. Vol. 2, New York, 1984.

———. *Jesus in the Eyes of the Sufis.* London, 1983

———. *In the Tavern of Ruin.* New York, 1978

Qoshairi, Abo'l-Qâsem. *Tarjoma'ye Resâla-ye Qoshairiya.* Edited by Badi'oz-Zamân' Foruzânfar. Tehran, 1982. In Persian.

Razi, Najmo'd-Din. *Merṣad al-'ebâd.* Edited by Moḥammad Amin Riyhi. Tehran, 1973. In Persian.

Rumi, Jalâlo'd-din. *Mathnawi-ye ma'nawi.* Edited by R. A. Nicholson. Fourth reprint, Tehran, 1977. In Persian.

Ruzbehân Baqli. *Mashrab al-arwaḥ.* Turkey: n.d. In Arabic.

———. *Sharḥ-e shaṭḥiyat.* Edited with notes, introduction, and indexes by Henry Corbin. Tehran. 1981. In Persian.

Sabzewâri, Ḥâj Mollâ Hâdi. *Diwân-e Ḥâj Mollâ Hâdi Sabzewâri.* Edited by Seyyed Moḥammad Reza-Da'i Javâd. Eṣfahân, n.d. In Persian.

Sa'di, Shaikh Maslaho'd-Din. *Golestân.* Edited by Khalil Khaṭib-Rahbar. Tehran, 1969. In Persian.

———. *Bustân.* Edited by Noro'llâh Irânparast. Tehran. 1989. In Persian.

———. *Kolliyât-e Sa'di.* Edited by Moḥammad 'Ali Forughi. Tehran. 1978. In Persian.

Sanâ'i, Ḥakim Abo'l-Majd Majdud. *Diwân.* Edited by Modarres Radhawi. Tehran, 1975. In Persian.

———. *Ḥadiqat al-ḥaqiqat wa shari'at aṭ-ṭariqat.* Edited by Modarres Radhawi. Tehran. 1950. In Persian.

Sarraj, Abu Naṣr at-Tusi as-. *Ketâb al-loma' fe't-taṣawwof.* E.J.W Gibb Memorial Series, No. 22, London, 1914. In Arabic.

Schimmel, Annemarie. *Mystical Dimensions of Islam.* Chapel Hill, U.S.A., 1975.

Shâh Ne 'mato'llâh Wali. *Resâlahâ-ye Shâh Ne'mato'llâh Wali.* Edited by Dr. Javad Nurbakhsh. 4 vols. Tehran, 1978. In Persian.

Smith, Margaret. *Rabia, The Mystic And Her Fellow Saints in Islam.* Cambridge, 1928.

Sohrawardi, Shehabo'd-Din Yahyâ. *Majmu'aye Mosannefat Shaikh 'Eshrâq.* Edited by Henri Corbin. Vols. 1 and 2 in Arabic. Vol. 3: *Oeuvres en Persan.* Tehran and Paris, 1977.

Sohrawardi, Shehabo d-Din Abu Hafs 'Omar. *Awâref at-ma'âref.* Bulaq, Egypt, 1872-73 (in the margin of Ghazâli's *Eḥyâ' al-'olum ad-din).* In Arabic.

Solami, Abu Abdor-Rahman. *Kitâb ṭabaqât aṣ-ṣufiyyah.* Edited by Johannes Peterson. Leiden, 1960. In Arabic.

Soyuti, 'Abdo'r-Rahmân ebn Abi Bakr as-. *Al-jâme' aṣ-ṣaghir.* Edited By Ḥasan Zarruq, et al. Aleppo, 1969-77. In Arabic.

Tahânawi. Moḥammad A'lâ ebn 'Ali. *Kashshâf* 145
eṣṭelâḥât al-fonun. Edited by Moḥammad Wajih.
Abd al-Ḥaqq and Gholam Kadir. 2 vols. Calcutta,
1862. In Persian and Arabic.

INDEX OF NAMES

Abu ‘Omar. *See* Najid, Abu ‘Omar; Zojâji, Abu ‘Omar
Abu Sa‘id Abo’l-Khair (d. 1049), ix, 45, 47, 61, 101, 102, 104
Abu Sa‘id, *See* Kharrâz, Abu Sa‘id Aḥmad al-.
Abu Solaimân Dârâni (d. 820), 104
Abu Torâb. *See* Nakhshabi, Abu Torâb.
Aflâki, (d. 1354), 102
Aḥmad ebn Hanbal (d. 855), 88
‘Aino’l-Qoḍhat Hamadani (d. 1131), 108
‘Ali Sahl Eṣfahâni (d. 893), 20
Anṣâri, Khwâja ‘Abdo’llâh (d. 1089), ix, x, 8, 9, 21, 31, 32, 33, 34, 44, 45, 49, 54, 55, 57, 60, 88, 109-111, 130-131
Anṭâki, Aḥmad ebn ‘Aṣem, 30
Arberry, A.J., 116, 118
‘Aṭṭâr, Farido’d-Din (d. 1221), 8, 135, 136
Avicenna (Ibn Sinâ) (d. 1037), 6, 71
Bâkhzari, Abo’l-Mofâkher Yaḥyâ (d. 1190), 35
Bâbâ Ṭâher Oryân Hamadâni (early llth century), x, 25, 26, 57, 58, 84, 107, 108
Bâyazid Bistâmi (d. 874), 53,
Ba Ya‘qub Mozâbeli, 57
Burckhardt, T, 126, 128
Corbin, H., 68,
Culme-Seymour, A., 126
Darrâj (d. 914), 26
Daqqâq, Abu ‘Ali (d. 1021), 10, 77, 97, 105, 130
Dinwari, Abu Bakr Moḥammad Dâwud Daqqi (d.937), 22, 77, 97, 130
Ebn ‘Arabi, Moḥya’d-Din Moḥammad (d. 1240), 126, 127
Ebn Jalâ (d. 918), 18, 54
Ebrâhim al-Qaṣṣâr (d. 938), 11
‘Ebrâhim ebn Adham (d. 776 or 783), 15
‘Erâhim ebn Khawâṣṣ (d. 904), 15
‘Eraqi, Fakhro’d-Din (d. 1289), 129
‘Ezzo’d-Din Maḥmud Kâshâni (d. 1334), 37, 78, 85, 87, 97, 112-114
Faḍhl Balkhi, Moḥammad ebn (d. 913), 25
Fâṭema Naishâburi (d. 849), 60

Maulânâ Jalâlo'd-Din Rumi. *See* Rumi, Maulâna Jalalo'd-Din.
Meṣri, Abu Bakr (d. 956), 21
Mobârak, Abu Moḥammad 'Abdo'llâh ebn (d.797), 103
Moḥammad, the Prophet (d. 632), 15, 9, 32, 34, 68, 78, 93, 135
Mohammad. *See* Faḍhl Balkhi, Moḥammad ebn; Ghazâli, Moḥammad; Ward, Moḥammad ebn Abo'l
Moḥâsebi, Ḥareth (d. 857), 78, 87
Morta'esh (d. 939), 12, 19, 58
Moses, 5, 109, 110, 130, 131
Moẓaffar Kermânshâhi, 20, 21, 55, 106
Mozaiyen, Abo'l-Ḥasan (d. 939), 20
Naishaburi, Abu Ḥafṣ. *See* Ḥaddâd, Abu Ḥafṣ.
Najid, Abu 'Omar, 77
Najmo'd -Din Kobra (d. 1220), 68, 86, 101
Nakhshabi, Abu Torâb (d. 859), 15
Naqshbandi, 42
Naṣrâbâdi, Abo'l-Qasem (d. 977), 55
Naṣr ebn Ḥammâmi, 22
Nezâmi, Ilyâs ebn Yusef (d. 1209), 124
Nicholson, R.A., 93, 102
Nojaid, Abu 'Omar ebn (d. 907), 77
Nuri, Abo'l-Ḥasan (d.907), 19, 61
Pearson, N., 68
Qaderi, 42
Qoshairi, Abo'l-Qâsem 'Abdo'l-Karim (d. 1072), x, 67, 74-75, 106, 123
Râbe'a al-'Adawiyya (d. 752 or 796 or 801), 18
Raḍhi, Abu 'Abdo'llâh, 28
Râzi, Shaikh Abo'l-Qâsem Maqarri, 56
Rowaim, Abu Moḥammad (d. 915), 10, 11, 56
Rudbâri, Abu 'Ali (d. 934), 16
Rumi, Maulânâ Jalâlo'd-Din (d. 1273), 28, 46, 47, 48, 88, 99, 101, 102, 103, 135
Ruzbehân Baqli (d. 1209), x, 29, 59, 60, 68, 70, 72, 73, 77, 79, 85, 101, 102, 108, 115-118, 132-133
Sabzewâri. *See* Ḥâj Mollâ Hâdi,
Sa'dân, Abu Bakr Abi, 21, 55